the air; when you're a little early, the tendency is to hit it on the ground toward some Golden Glove infielder. Just knowing that basic fact puts you ahead of the game. Mel Ott, another little guy, hit over 500 home runs, and he gave most of the credit to timing.

Results Are What Count

If this were a recipe book, I guess you'd just mix those five ingredients together, put them in the oven at 350 degrees, and cook up a great hitter. Well obviously it doesn't work that way. While many players may possess some — or even all — of the qualities that I just identified, only a very select few make full use of them throughout their careers. A bad chef might have the best ingredients in the world, but the results can still prove disastrous.

After all, baseball is not a neat cause-and-effect kind of game. You can't apply a formula — great eyesight + great power + intelligence + courage + timing = a great hitter — to baseball. It's not an exact science. There are still things like heart and desire and dedication and hard work that enter into the equation too. Sometimes a player with only mediocre natural talent can out-perform a guy with a ton of God-given ability. I've seen it many times.

That's why the proof of the hitter is in the numbers. Statistics and career records provide concrete, irrefutable evidence of those who were best able to take full advantage of their ability over the long haul. And while it's perfectly true that statistics don't tell the whole story and are incapable of measuring intangibles like heart and desire, they can provide you with a yard-stick to compare the results of a hitter's skill and effort. I'll talk more later about the statistical process that was used to help compile the Hit List and establish the rankings.

THE RANKINGS

I've come to the conclusion that if hitting a baseball is the most difficult thing to do in sport, then getting two people to agree on who did it best must be a close second. Even if it is possible to identify the top 25 hitters of all time more or less accurately, you'd almost think you were defying the baseball deities the way people react when you try to put them in some actual ranking. Fans take these things seriously, and I know how many pitfalls there are in an undertaking like this.

After all, how much drop-off is there from a Cadillac to the very best Buick? There's a little drop-off, but they're still the same basic luxury car. These are good, but those are the best, that's what it comes down to. And that's what I've done to create the Hit List. After thorough study and careful scrutiny, I've come up with a list of the players that I am convinced are the 25 greatest hitters of all time.

From the first time I swung a bat back in San Diego, throughout my minor and major league career, and during my time as a manager and batting instructor, I've tried to learn all I could about hitters and hitting. I never passed up an opportunity to talk with my contemporaries from both leagues, or with those great old-timers whose eyes lit up when they recalled a Cobb slide or a long homer by the Babe. Even today, if a bright young prospect is genuinely interested and wants to bend my ear on my favorite subject, I won't say no.

I've questioned, I've probed, I've challenged, I've argued, and in my early years I probably made a genuine nuisance of myself with my persistence. But the most important thing I did was listen. And I was a pretty good listener, too. I knew I had a lot to learn, and I couldn't learn it fast enough for my liking. Those conversations were usually focused on the techniques of hitting, but invariably at some point the discussion would come around to specific hitters — what they did and how they did it.

I talked at length with Cobb and with Hornsby and Collins and a host of other early legends of the game, and I drew heavily on those memorable conversations when the time came to evaluate the dead ball era hitters for my Hit List. I was always jawing with Joe Cronin, who had a broad knowledge of players from his era and before. And I still talk occasionally with Musial and DiMaggio and Berra and an all-star lineup of other former major leaguers. They all have strong opinions — opinions that can't be ignored.

I know that my choices are not necessarily the same as yours, and that I'll never succeed in converting some of you to my way of thinking. Sure, I have some significant advantages when evaluating the talent of this and other eras. Hell, I was right there on the field for much of it and saw many of those guys up close. For well over 50 years I've been steeped in the practice and the lore of hitting. For many of us, however, rankings are devised as much in the heart as in the head. While I tend to be purely analytical when ranking the great hitters, there is an emotional element at work when people defend their favorite players, and God knows those choices are none the less valid for that. Perhaps you saw Mickey Mantle electrify a Yankee Stadium crowd by hitting a tape-measure home run one warm summer day when you were safe in the crook of your father's arm — one of those days when all was right with the world. Or it could be your Italian heritage that caused you to worship the great Joe DiMaggio, although just watching him go from first to third on a single would be enough for me. That was a thing of beauty. Remember that great little book by Hemingway, *The Old Man and the Sea*? The old fisherman, Santiago, liked DiMaggio because he had read somewhere that Joe's father was also a commercial fisherman. If you have a common bond of experience, the best statistical evidence in the world won't change your mind.

Maybe your ancestors hailed from Krakow or Warsaw and those Polish ties caused your pulse to quicken whenever Stan Musial or Yaz strode to the plate. It could be anything — a steadfast loyalty to a particular player's era or team or hometown can inspire your choices. That's the way it should be, and it doesn't have to be analyzed or defended.

Still, it always amazes me the way fans relate so strongly to a certain player, and the way those people come from all sectors of society. NBC sportscaster Bob Costas isn't ashamed to admit that he carries a Mantle baseball card wherever he goes. Conservative commentator and *Newsweek* columnist George Will puts aside weightier subjects to write an eloquent tribute to the batting consistency of Wade Boggs. Meanwhile, actor Dabney Coleman has written a nice piece in *Inside Sport* related to my hitting abilities, and his former TV persona, Slap Maxwell, used to invoke the spirit of Teddy Ballgame whenever he faced a personal crisis. It might have been a bit premature, but I appreciated the thought nonetheless.

Given this loyalty to particular players, it isn't surprising that argument is a big part of the allure of baseball. What was the greatest team ever? Who was the fastest pitcher? The slickest-fielding second baseman? Those kinds of questions are all fuel for the hot-stove league. But without a doubt the facet of the game that produces the loudest arguments is hitting. Who were the greatest hitters of all time? It's a debate that will continue to rage as long as baseball holds sway over the youth of this country, which I hope is for a long time to come.

This book will no doubt fuel a lot more argument. I hope it does. In fact, if it doesn't generate argument — and lots of it — it has probably failed in its purpose. Not that anything was deliberately done to cause such disagreement. No artificial controversy was built into the text to boost sales. I had my fair share of controversy in my playing days and I sure wouldn't go out of my way to create more at this point in my life. That's hardly necessary when everyone is so dead sure in his or her heart who the great hitters were — and who they were not. Still, baseball wouldn't be nearly as much fun if everyone cheered for the same heroes.

Let's face it, there has never been a perfect hitter. Ruth and Mantle struck out too much, and Cobb was a push hitter with no power. The two who would appear to have everything are Rogers Hornsby and Shoeless Joe. They didn't seem to have any real flaws, but I could point to every hitter I personally saw, including Ted Williams, and tell you where they fell short of their potential — every hitter I saw, including the greatest hitters I saw play. The only thing you can do is to investigate and find out who, for whatever reasons, made the best use of their talents.

That's why it's important for the reader to know that while this book is written from a hitter's perspective, and with a hitter's background and in-

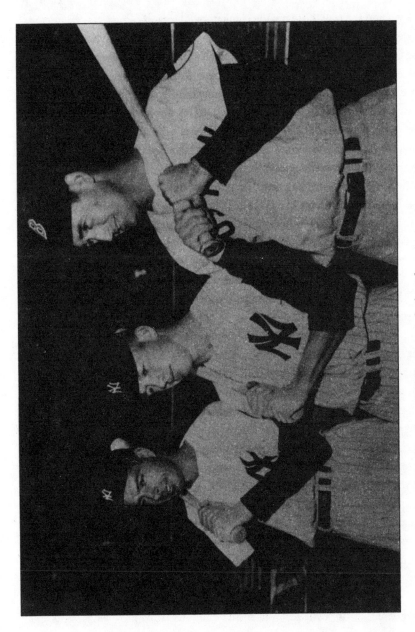

DiMaggio, Mantle, and Williams: a pitcher's nightmare. H.V. PAT REILLY, WYCKOFF, N.J.

sights, it also incorporates a reliable statistical system to help validate each selection and assist us in the ranking of the top 25 hitters.

For comparison purposes, *Ted Williams' Hit List* used a publication called *Total Baseball*, by John Thorn and Pete Palmer, as our major source for statistical data. It's a comprehensive work and has served as our reference throughout this project. Not only does *Total Baseball* provide the more traditional statistics, such as batting averages, slugging percentages, home run and RBI totals, but it also features a smorgasbord of less traditional, but in many ways more revealing, stats.

Of those statistics related solely to hitting, I give special credence to one used by Thorn and Palmer, known as production. Production (PRO.) is determined by adding on base percentage (OBP) and slugging average (SLG.). On base percentage is a stat developed by Roth and Rickey in the early '50s. It is arrived at by calculating hits plus walks plus hit by pitch and dividing by at-bats plus walks plus hit by pitch. Slugging average, of course, is determined by dividing total bases by at-bats. We looked at various systems and methods, and we can't conceive of anything superior to this one. It is a simple statistic that is nonetheless as fair, as thorough, and as thought-out as any that has ever been used.

Production is the bottom line in hitting and that's why production is our bottom-line stat. It's a great indicator, a great yardstick of hitting. It also serves as an equalizer, a tool for making valid comparisons of hitters from various eras and for evaluating what a particular hitter has accomplished across his career. This single statistic most closely reflects my thinking on what makes up a superior hitter.

I realize that everyone has a different idea of what constitutes a great hitter. For some it's a high batting average. For others it's the guy with the most total hits — or home runs, or RBIs. I've always believed that slugging percentage plus on base percentage is absolutely the best way to rate the hitters. This is something I've been talking about for a long, long time. To begin with, I've always felt that the bases on balls factor should be given more significance in rating a hitter's overall performance at the plate. When I played, walks weren't counted nearly as much as they are now. Now they're starting to talk about it a little differently.

Even today, though, few people really realize the importance of those 125 extra bases. They only count the hits — the home runs and the doubles and triples. Well, let me tell you, a great hitter should walk three times for every strikeout. If a hitter like Don Mattingly isn't walking, he knows he's hitting too many pitchers' pitches. So I'm thrilled to see that they're finally starting to recognize the importance of the walk. I think it's overdue, you're damn right I do.

Total bases is the key. Production is the key. I have tried to take as my credo the belief that the best hitter is the most productive one. All you have to do to find the most productive hitters is start with the guys who get the most total bases and go from there. That's why the production stat is the best overall gauge of a hitter there is. It doesn't fail and it hasn't failed us.

Total Baseball actually carries it one step further to create a stat called adjusted production, which takes into account home park characteristics that help or hurt a batter, and league average. For our purposes I have ignored this variation, choosing instead to make those adjustments based on my own knowledge of ballparks, styles, and other, more subjective hitters' yardsticks. Some of these are very hard, if not impossible, to quantify, and you can't apply them to any neat formula, but I will speak in general terms later about many of those "compensating factors" that affect a player's performance. Hopefully they will serve to explain some of the apparent contradictions between the production numbers and the actual rankings.

In order to conduct any kind of fair comparisons, we must place the hitters on an equal footing. To the casual observer Pete Rose might appear to have an edge on Ty Cobb, because Rose sprayed out more base hits than any other player. However, when you consider that Rose was at bat almost 3000 more times than Cobb, and still finished his career with only 64 more lifetime hits, you start to see things a bit differently. Obviously it's important wherever possible to avoid comparing apples and oranges. On closer inspection Cobb was a bona fide Georgia Peach, while a Rose is a Rose is a Rose.

That's why one logical starting point is to measure accomplishments on a per-time-at-bat basis. I think that what a guy does per time at bat is very significant. You can never make me believe Mays and Aaron were better than Ruth and Gehrig and DiMaggio based on per times at bat. Mays and Aaron, and even Musial — and certainly Rose and Yastrzemski — are from an era of players whose careers weren't interrupted by service in the armed forces. They had a chance to carry on and play those extra four or five years, and then they started seeing goals that they could attain because of their longevity. And you sure have to say one thing: They had longevity! But when you start comparing them with the Ruths and Gehrigs per time at bat, it's right out the window with those guys.

Among those whose ranking was negatively affected by a limited number of at-bats was Hank Greenberg. Based solely on his production stats, Greenberg should have been fourth on our list instead of eleventh. However,

Hank was only up 5000-odd times. Through no fault of his own, his career was cut short by the Second World War, and he was never the same after the war. So despite his great production numbers, I was compelled to move him down.

My ideal cutoff point for times at bat I would put at about 6500. Ideally, a guy would have to be up 6500-7000 times. Greenberg is a borderline case because of his time in the service. I lost four and one-half years of a career and I only got up 7706 times, so I can sympathize. Also due to unusual circumstances, Joe Jackson fell well short of 6500, as did Kiner, Klein and Mize. It's impossible to project what they might have done if they had played a full, uninterrupted career. They might have maintained those high levels throughout, or they might have started to fade anyway. Based on what I saw and heard about these individuals, I think they would have continued to dominate pitchers. But we'll never know.

We also gave considerable weight to the more traditional statistics. This explains another apparent contradiction. Some of Willie Mays' records — including production — are slightly more impressive than Aaron's. But Aaron hit more home runs than anyone else. That counts for a hell of a lot and has to be factored in. You can't ignore a feat like that. Those two guys were extremely tough to rank, but sometimes you have to go with your gut feeling and your own personal observations. In the case of National Leaguers, I often consulted former players from that league, guys who saw Mays and Aaron up close on a regular basis.

Mantle was another player who could well have been placed higher, except for what I saw as an unwillingness to make adjustments at the plate according to the count. With his talent, he might have been better than any of them. I really believe he had enough going for him: speed, power, the whole enchilada. I certainly have no hesitation in calling him the greatest switch-hitter who ever lived.

Batting averages were also considered. A lot of researchers may disagree with me, but whereas a hit total can be deceptive because of varying number of at-bats, an average tells you something. Unless he has other outstanding credentials, anyone who doesn't hit .300 is not, in my book, a truly great hitter. I really can't believe that he is. That's one of the guidelines for selection. A .295 hitter would be considered in the top thirty — and then if you're not happy with someone else in there, you'd have to consider moving him up. I consider .300 to be a significant threshold for a hitter but those who fall short of the mark would get special consideration if they dominated in another hitting category. The glaring exceptions to this rule of thumb are

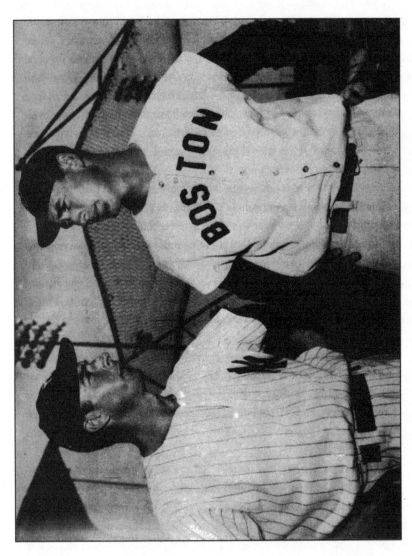

DiMaggio and Williams: the hottest rivalry in baseball. AP/WIDE WORLD PHOTOS

Ralph Kiner, Mike Schmidt, Harmon Killebrew and Willie McCovey. But then Kiner, a lifetime .279 hitter, boasts the second-best home run frequency in baseball history, and Schmidt, a .267 hitter, hit 542 homers and owned National League pitchers for years. Likewise, Killebrew batted a paltry .256 but also powered 573 home runs, and McCovey's .270 was more than made up for by his 521 homers.

So an average is just another tool, and I sure don't consider a .300 average in itself as the criterion of who is the greatest hitter. There are countless numbers of high-average hitters who didn't come anywhere near the list: Carew, Boggs, and so on. But when you have all those other statistics — 1700, 1800, 1900 RBIs, 575 or 600 home runs, or at least 500-plus — then you've got to consider that guy.

Ernie Banks wouldn't be considered because he was not a .300 hitter (.274 lifetime) and his production numbers were also relatively low — even though he hit 512 home runs and led the league twice. Eddie Matthews has a similar career average (.271) and the same number of homers but his superior production elevates him to the Honorable Mention category.

So almost all the guys we're talking about are .300 hitters. Maybe .290 is close enough for me, but not much lower, unless there are compensating factors which can't be ignored. Killebrew is the best example of a player with a low average and a high home run count. Sure Killebrew was a one-dimensional hitter. He was a slugger. But, oh what a slugger he was!

I don't pay quite as much attention to RBI totals because opportunity is what counts there. I had guys drive in as many runs as me who had 50 percent more chances to drive in a run, so it's deceptive.

The statistical criteria that we used to determine the top 25 hitters, therefore, include total bases and performance on a per-time-at-bat basis — in short, production. But as I've said, there are other considerations. You have to temper statistics with common sense and personal observation, otherwise you could list the top 25 production figures and close the book on the subject. Well, it ain't that simple.

Baseball is unique in a number of ways. Unlike football gridirons or basketball courts, no two baseball fields have the same dimensions, which obviously can have a huge effect on a player's offensive numbers, especially home runs. And then there have been changes in the ball, and in gloves and other equipment, which have had an impact on the efficiency with which the game is played. And night games and airplane travel and domed stadiums and artificial turf . . . an infinite number of factors that affect a hitter's performance and make fair comparisons especially difficult.

On the following pages I offer some thoughts on many of these compensating factors. I do this mainly by drawing on experiences from my own career, and I relate these personal anecdotes only to help illustrate the kinds of problems faced by hitters. Baseball is a flesh-and-blood game, and while statistics provide a standard of achievement, the game shouldn't — and can't — be reduced to a sterile numbers game. I hope that the point of view I offer will complement the wonderful research done by baseball historians.

The Ballpark Factor

What role do ballparks play in determining the success of a hitter? Did Home Run King Hank Aaron benefit from playing his career in so-called hitters' parks? Would I have been a better hitter, as some experts suggest, if I'd played in Yankee Stadium with its short right-field wall? Would DiMaggio, a right-handed batter, have produced better batting statistics in Fenway Park with that inviting Green Monster in left field?

Well, to begin with, I don't subscribe to the conventional wisdom that says DiMaggio and I should have switched parks, although I do think we would have done better in Detroit or Cleveland. How would I have fared in Yankee Stadium? I walked more times in Yankee Stadium than in any other place. For the 11 years that Casey Stengel managed the Yankee ballclub, there was a rule there that if Williams beats anybody in the seventh, eighth, or ninth inning, he'll get a fine. So you see, I didn't get as much to hit, although that's no excuse on my part.

I hit .305 in Yankee Stadium! And remember, I was walked more times in Yankee Stadium than in any other ballpark. Now back home at Fenway, I hit .365 against the Yankees lifetime, against the same pitchers, basically — but we had a pretty good supporting cast of right-handed hitters with that short porch to shoot at, so then those Yankee pitchers have got to pitch to you, and that made one hell of a difference. It's true that I had to hit about 400 feet at Fenway and about 310 in Yankee Stadium, but goddamn it, I had a hard time because I never got a very good ball to hit. As a result, I'd get to the plate in Yankee Stadium sometimes and just kind of relax and not really be ready and — Ball one! Ball two! — and heck, never get a pitch. And so I'd get lax sometimes. That's no excuse, it's the truth. You look and see how many times I walked in Yankee Stadium.

Hitters like Mel Ott are often criticized and their performance devalued because they played in friendly, and in some cases downright affectionate, ballparks. Statistics may not lie, but they don't always tell the whole truth either. Ott, for example, hit an inordinate 325 of his 511 home runs in a New York bandbox called the Polo Grounds where a 250-foot fly ball was a round-tripper. But give him his due. Ott was smart, too; he learned to adjust to his ballpark environment better than anyone else could.

The truly great hitters could hit anywhere, as indicated by this chart of DiMaggio, Mays, and Aaron:

	AB	AVG.	SLG.	OBP	HR	RBI	PRO.
DiMaggio							
Home	3360	.315	.546	.391	148	720	.938
Away	3461	.333	.610	.405	213	817	1.015
Mays							
Home	5239	.302	.567	.389	335	930	.955
Away	5642	.301	.549	.385	325	973	.934
Aaron							
Home	5972	.303	.556	.382	385	1117	.939
Away	6392	.306	.553	.372	370	1180	.925

AB — At-Bats; AVG. — Batting Average; SLG. — Slugging Percentage; OBP — On Base Percentage; HR — Home Runs; RBI — Runs Batted In; PRO. — Production

If hitters were hired to design ballparks in the manner that Jack Nicklaus designs championship golf courses, what would they look like? Well, if I were the architect they would start with damn good lights. Good background. Sometimes at night you can have a better background than you have in the daytime. In some cases you don't really have to have a background at all at night because the lights are so well located. The Baltimore ballpark was terrible when the Orioles first entered the league. It was far better hitting at night than in the daytime, because there was a white school out there beyond the outfield, and their organization didn't do a damn thing about it. Just terrible! And I can tell you other ballparks where the shadows get long and it gets tough. I'd rather hit at night in those parks.

We always had a pretty good background in Fenway Park. That's the reason people like to hit there. A lot of the parks had really good backgrounds: Detroit, Cleveland. Yankee Stadium, not so good. Of course, it always affects the visiting team more than it affects the home team. I can remember people saying that when there was a big crowd at Fenway, they thought the background was bad. It never bothered me because I was used to it, but with a lefthander pitching to a right-handed hitter, I know damn well it'd be tough.

A good hitter has to adapt himself a little bit to where he's playing. For instance, Vic Wertz played for Detroit, which has a short right field. He crowded the plate. We used to crowd him, pitch him high and tight, and he'd miss and swing a little late and get out. Every once in a while he'd crank one, but he wasn't a good hitter at that point. Then they traded him to Cleveland.

Cleveland was a bigger park, harder to hit in, and when he got there he must have said to himself, "No use in me trying to pull the ball. I'm going to get off the plate." And he became a hell of a hitter — a hell of a hitter! — hitting the ball a little more away from him and not trying to pull it. He sparked Cleveland to a pennant in 1954. Later he came to our ballclub and he was still a hell of a hitter. It just goes to show that hitters have to adjust not only to pitchers and counts but also to the unique character of the ballpark.

Everyone always thought that Griffith Stadium in Washington was a tough park to hit in. Well, hell, I loved to hit in Washington! The ball flew out of there and it looked like I was hitting downhill all the time. Some parks hit you in a different way. I always thought that the damn pitcher looked four feet closer to me in Philadelphia's Shibe Park than in any other place — but still I used to hit like hell there. In fact I went six for eight in Shibe Park to clinch .400 on the last day of the '41 season, so obviously I liked the place.

Another thing. You've got to make the home run distances reasonable! There are things in every ballpark that make it a little uncomfortable or that make it enjoyable, but most importantly you've got to be able to see the ball and you've got to have the fences reachable. Don't give the pitcher that much advantage. Hell, he doesn't need that much advantage. He's got eight guys out there and you don't need to have the fences 400 feet in every direction. I'd say down the line 335 feet, through the middle alleys 380 feet, and centerfield 405 to 410 feet. Now those are reasonable distances, but you've still got to hit the ball well for it to go out.

Domes are a necessary evil, especially in those major league cities with less temperate climes. I suspect that Montreal and Toronto both qualify — although it gets pretty cold in Detroit and Chicago and they still play outside. However, indoor or out, the dimensions must be fair. The big fault of domes is that most of them are not designed well for baseball. Houston, for example, was hurt, and will be hurt forever perhaps, and may even end up leaving the Astrodome, because the place isn't as fair a facility as it should have been. They have the fences located where Babe Ruth couldn't hit one out, and they've made a pitcher's paradise out of it. They may have straightened it out some now, though. Apparently the Seattle and Minnesota domes are both easy to hit in.

The Pitching Factor
Impact of the Slider

They talk about the slider as if it's a new invention that only the modern hitters have to struggle with. I started in 1939 and the slider was first thrown in 1947, so for about eight or nine years of my 22-year span in the big leagues I didn't have to face the slider, but I had the slider all the rest of those years. It really started to take over in '47, and in '48 certainly it was prevalent. Hell, yes — and from 1948 on I looked for the sliders, and I keyed my hitting on them.

I knew I could hit a fastball with anybody, but because every pitcher started to add the slider to their repertoire, I had to make that adjustment. Why? Because it was harder for me to hit the slider if I was looking for a fastball, harder to pull it and really get it in the air, than it was for me to look for the slider and adjust to the fastball and get that pitch in the air.

I really didn't give a damn if I hit it to right field. As long as I hit it good, I knew I could hit it out: left center, centerfield, or wherever the hell it was. So I had a much better chance of doing that if I was looking for the slider. And another thing. Looking for a slider made me wait a little longer, because the slider is a little slower pitch. If I'd keyed on the fastball and then gotten a slider, I'd be sure to hit a ground ball, and I sure didn't want to do that. Ground balls were nothing to me! They were outs! They had the defense stacked against me and they had all kinds of exaggerated shifts devised to stop me — and I sure couldn't beat anything out with my speed. From second base to home I had average speed, but when I took a good hard rip at the ball I'd fall toward third, and so I had a disadvantage going down the line to first. Those are all reasons why I decided to key on the slider.

A slider just gives the pitcher a third pitch, like in the old shell game. You can take two walnuts, and the guy gives you the fast moves with the walnuts and you don't even have to look, and you pick a walnut and you'll be right 50 percent of the time. But you put that third walnut in there and then you start guessing, because you don't know where it is. Your chances of guessing right immediately go down to 33 percent. That's why, for batters, the advent of the slider made a huge difference. If a pitcher relies on two main pitches, you're guessing right 50 percent of the time. What the hell, you may get five pitches in a given at-bat. All you've got to do is get one good pitch and guess right and get it in the right spot, and you should hit it pretty well. A good, experienced hitter will lay for it and jump on that one good pitch he sees. When you add the slider to the mix, your odds drop by a third and the pressure is really on to cash in on that one pitch.

So that's what the slider did. It gave every pitcher another pitch. It's not a curve, it's not a fastball, it's a slider. It's easy to learn how to pitch, and easier to control than a breaking ball. So right away that put another thing in the pitcher's arsenal. The impact on hitters was so great that ten years later they finally had to do something to try to help them, and that's when they dropped the pitching mound.

Mays called it the toughest pitch he faced; so did Aaron. The hitters were really suffering, and you know what happened when they dropped the mound? There were a couple of records set in the league, and everybody was hitting about 30 points higher right off the bat. That's how big an impact one phase of the game can have on hitters.

Those are all things that baseball fans should keep in mind. All those changes and refinements had an impact on hitters. Just as the fans should know that the lively ball was introduced in 1920. Ruth couldn't have hit 50 home runs in the dead ball era. The year he jumped to 54 home runs from 11 and 29 the previous two years, that signaled the advent of the lively ball era and changed baseball from a game of finesse to a game of finesse and power. The introduction of the slider was another one of those checks and balances that keep the batter or the pitcher from getting the upper hand.

The Forkball

Today pitchers make much more use of the forkball. It's become a reliable pitch for many of them. There were always guys who had some success with it — Elroy Face was one — but the big thing about the forkball is that it's hard to get it over the damn plate. And a 102-mile-per-hour fastball is hard to get over the plate! The wonderful thing about this game is that there are so many compensating factors. The guy with the tremendous exploding curve can't get the darn thing over and the guy who doesn't have all that stuff can thread a needle. The guy with all the power in the world can't make contact and the guy who has wings doesn't have power.

The Spitball

Should the spitball be legalized? No. I think that it's dirty and the pitcher doesn't need it. I think those illegal pitches are more of a psychological factor than anything else. I think many hitters psyche themselves out. For some of them it's just an act to let everyone think they are psyched out, because they can't hit the damn thing anyway. You know those guys, wailing and moaning after striking out. It's a handy excuse.

The big thing is, they see all of those trick pitches, and you know what happens? They swing at bad balls all the time. Anything that's that hard to throw or is that good is also hard to get over. But they still swing at them. There is no question about it: the modern hitter swings at an awful lot of bad balls.

Pitchers: Ted's Personal Gallery of Greats

Different types of pitchers give trouble to different types of hitters. I can only speak for myself and offer some examples of pitchers who were damn tough on me. They were usually the smart pitchers, like Whitey Ford, Bob Feller, Hoyt Wilhelm, Bob Lemon. They all had different strengths but they all had that in common.

New York Yankee Spud Chandler was tough on me. He was like Cleveland's Bob Lemon. He had a hard sinkerball and kept the ball down. He was a little herky-jerky, had a good curveball — a real quick curve. He was a hard guy to pull for a left-hander. And of course Lemon was very close to the same type of pitcher.

You know a guy who should have been as tough as any of them? A guy named Donovan, Dick Donovan, but he went too much with that one pitch, the slider. He had a better slider than either one of those other guys, and he had as good a curveball as either, and darn near as good a fastball, but he went with that one pitch too much. Some pitchers do that. Donovan won 20 games one season, but he should have been a more consistent pitcher.

The Yankees' Whitey Ford was tough on me. Hell, he never struck me out, but I never felt that I could ever really rip on him. He always had the ball down and away, down and away, down and away — and then POP — he brought it in on you. Then down and away again. He had a good, quick little curve. He was a good little pitcher. And then you take guys like Wilhelm,

Lopat, a fellow named Scarborough who had a tough, hard curve. Those kinds of pitchers are still around today and still darn successful. Smart, crafty guys like Jimmy Key. Key looks real good to me. He would have been tough on me. He's a left-hander and he's got a good delivery, a tough, high, three-quarter delivery.

For speed I'd single out Trucks, I think. Virgil Trucks and Bob Feller were the Roger Clemens and Randy Johnson of that period. You say them in the same breath for speed. But when you talk about the greatest pitcher, there's no question: it has to be the Cleveland Indians' Bob Feller. He had a hell of a curveball. Herky-jerky. He was the kind of fellow that when he came into town everybody got geared up, because they knew they were going to see Mr. Feller. I think when you say that, you can see he had a great influence on the players of the day. They were going to see Feller, something a little extra was going to happen that day. And it always did.

At that time they pitched differently to me than to anyone else on the Red Sox club. I would see the first knuckleball the opposing pitcher had, or the first screwball, or the first slider. A guy would come back to the bench and he'd say, "Goddamn, that guy threw me a slider." And I would be saying to myself, "Hell, he threw them to me last year!" Or a knuckleball, or anything else. They used to try things out on me, experiment on me. The big hitters always get that kind of special attention from pitchers. It's like a challenge for both of them, a showdown — gunfight at the OK Corral.

I once struck out on a knuckleball and everyone on our bench laughed. A little pudgy Cuban guy who smoked big cigars was pitching — I can't remember his name. Hellfire, he threw me three great knucklers and I swung and missed and I struck out. My teammates were all kind of laughing. We had a good lead, but I said, "Don't laugh, that S.O.B. is tougher than you think." They didn't know anything about him. But they soon found out.

I used to watch all these opposing pitchers in the bullpen. They were always playing around and experimenting. They show you what they've got in the bullpen because they want to throw everything they've got and work on certain pitches and all the rest. I was well aware of those pitches a lot of times. I can think distinctly of Detroit, where I was in left field and they'd be warming up out there, and I could see them and see everything that was going on. So I had a pretty good insight as to the type of pitcher a guy was. That's what good hitters have to do if they want to stay ahead of the game.

The Bat, the Ball, and the Modern Hitter
Corked Bats

Blaming corked bats too much for the increase in hitting is just wrong. It's insignificant. They caught Cleveland's Albert Belle a while back and made a big deal of it. Let me tell you something: they are trying to make a lot of excuses for a goddamn lively ball. The big thing is, you can hit with a piece of banana wood or you can hit with a piece of dynamite, but you've still got to make contact and you've got to hit it on the good part of the bat. I think this business of the corked bats is way, way, way overexploited and bellyached about. Hellfire, it doesn't mean a thing. Now if the ball has been tampered with, that's a different thing.

Lighter Bats

Everybody asks why the hell I was so quick with the bat. I was pretty strong, not beastly strong, but mainly I was quick. You know why I was so damn quick? I want to tell you something: I had the lightest bat in the league for maximum strength per pound. And it started a trend toward light bats.

I had to laugh because in 1960 someone in the media brought up the fact that all of a sudden everybody's hitting for higher averages and all the rest of it. Willie Mays came out and he said, "Well, I have a lighter bat this year." And I thought, Well isn't that funny? Old Ted had it 22 years before. As Casey Stengel would say, "You can look it up." Today's players use much lighter bats.

Cobb used a heavy bat, a 40-ouncer, but even he made the move to a lighter model later on in his career. Ruth used barge poles, though! Some of his bats were 50 ounces or more. Musial's were about like mine.

On Patience

So many guys are swinging when they leave the bench. All you do when you do that is hit the pitcher's pitch, and don't you think the pitcher knows that? The pitcher says, "Hell, I'm not giving these guys anything to hit till I have to." So what's happening? The batter's getting something tough all the time.

The thing is, I always got criticized for taking a pitch an inch or an inch and a half off the plate. Nowadays when hitters do that they've got "great patience." And yet they were always lambasting me. Cobb got on

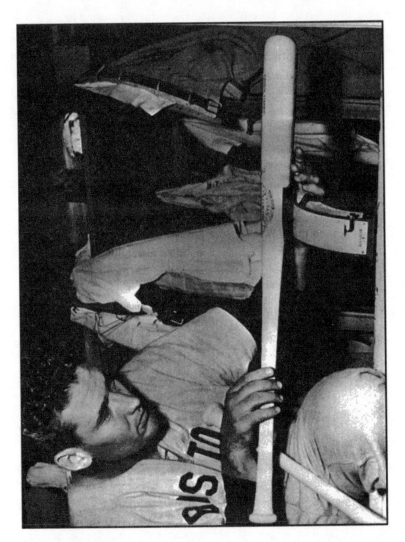

Ted and the tools of his trade. COLLECTION OF BRIAN INTERLAND

me for that. And why Ty Cobb would do that I don't know except that he was a strange guy.

Now when they first asked me to compare Boggs and Mattingly, I said they have to give the edge to Mattingly because because at that time he was hitting 25-30 homers every year and Boggs was hitting about seven. But I now know that Boggs is a much better hitter — day in and day out. In my estimation Mattingly failed to progress and began to go back as a hitter. He started to give the bat that little curl and he's not as smart at the plate. Boggs is a very smart hitter. He makes the pitcher pitch. If he's fooled, he doesn't fool with the pitch. When he's got two strikes, he'll go inside-out, inside-out. He has that great facility of hitting with two strikes. He doesn't strike out much. He's right there all the time. Not only does he concede with two strikes, he concedes with one strike, and that's why he doesn't hit the long ball. But then again, we're not talking about those guys for this list.

The Modern Hitter

It's easy to criticize the modern player, but I always said I wasn't going to do that. The only real criticism that I've ever leveled at Boggs or Rod Carew — outstanding hitters, outstanding hitters — is that in batting practice, Boggs will put a hell of a long ball show on for you in the bleachers, but in a game — phip! phip! phip! — he just tries to spray the ball. Well, batting practice and a game are exactly the same! You gear yourself up a little bit and, hell, if you can hit those balls in practice, you should be able to hit them in the game. And yet it doesn't happen. Don't ask me why.

That would be my only criticism, because they have already proved they can do it and yet they don't try. With two strikes, of course let 'em do it that way, but when you've got the count in your favor, when you've got a certain kind of pitcher, when you've got the wind, when you've got the park, when you've got the game on the line — the type of game where you want to try to crank one — do it!

I thought Boggs was capable of 20 home runs a year and I thought that George Brett was capable of 20 home runs a year (and that's when he wasn't hitting them). Carew hit 20 one year and never hit that many again. The only year Boggs did it was when they livened up the ball in 1987 and he responded with 24 homers. Since then he's only hit ten or 12.

Some readers might question the scarcity of modern day players on the Hit List. All I can say is that they were examined with the same scrutiny as the older players, and the rules for them today are the same as the rules for those guys then. They have been rated according to the same guidelines. In order to make any fair assessment, you really have to look at a player's total career. However, there are some excellent candidates waiting — guys with names like Thomas, and Griffey, Jr., and Bonds and Gwynn and Bagwell and Williams — who need only continue what they're doing.

The Geography of Hitting
The Russians Aren't Coming!

A few years ago, the Canadian hockey establishment and the NHL made the mistake of underestimating the Russians as an emerging hockey power. The Russians have also produced some pretty fair basketball players. But you can bet your ass they will never become a baseball threat, despite some growing interest in the sport. You can bet it won't amount to anything.

Their weather's lousy as I understand it. Cold. You could play three months of the year at most. There is no way you are going to compete against kids playing nine, ten, or even 12 months of the year in other countries. No way, no way! Why? Because the single hardest thing to do in sport is hit a baseball, and the way you excel most prominently and most effectively is by being able to hit.

The reason there aren't more Canadians in the major leagues is that — as I've said a million times — hitting a baseball is the hardest thing to do in sport, and in a place like Canada you get to hit only a fraction as much as I did when I played every month and every day of the year in San Diego. They have more time to play hockey and they're better at it than we are. But in baseball you need all the time and every opportunity to play and hit. So it's understandable that hitting is hard for Canadians and Russians.

That's why a little country like the Dominican Republic produces so many fine players. Their weather allows them to play a lot of baseball. Period. They are light and quick and and they gravitate to the infield where they cash in on that stuff. The Cubans are heavier and they produce more power hitters.

I don't know how you can make adjustments for cold weather. It's a pain in the ass and I never did like it. God, I hated cold weather. I couldn't get loose and I just didn't feel hitterish! It's just a hell of a lot tougher to hit when it's cold and it's a lot easier for the pitcher. He shouldn't get tired and he should be able to stay warm. And don't forget, when it gets cold you are usually hitting against a prevailing wind that's always blowing in.

That's why Harmon Killebrew's record is so impressive. Now he was a strong fellow, but he's from Idaho, for Pete's sake, with Idaho's bad weather, and yet he hit more home runs in the American League than any other right-handed batter who ever lived.

It requires total commitment to overcome disadvantages like that! That is why people come out to the major league parks to see it done well. The hitters are what you talk about. Take Roberto Alomar, for example. He's a great little second baseman and he's fun to watch, but it's still the hitters that people pay to see; it's the hitters that they talk about on the drive home.

Runs, Hits, and ERAs

It would have been tempting to qualify the selections for the Hit List by dividing the choices into neat little compartments: best "dead ball" era hitters and best post-1920 "lively ball" hitters, or pre-1969 and post-1969. It certainly would have made the task much simpler, and in some ways it would have made for a fairer basis for comparison. But ultimately, I believe, it would have been a cop-out.

After all, when you talk about the great orators of history, you don't divide them into the pre- and post-television days, the Churchill era and the Kennedy era. When you rank the great singers of all time, you don't make allowances based on the style of music they played or the outmoded sentiments sometimes expressed in the songs. Surely greatness in sport, as in all things, rises above the eccentricities of a particular era, and a Cobb, Ruth, or Joe Jackson would have been a bona fide star in any era. Sure it was a different game, with different demands on the players. But the true greats were so talented and so driven that they could have adapted their skills to the conventions of any era.

One of the many great things about the game of baseball is the sense of continuity and history that it has carefully preserved. Unlike many sports, baseball is rooted in its history. The diamond heroes of yesterday are still revered and they provide the standards by which the next generation is judged. It's all connected and it's what makes baseball unique. Each generation of ballplayers adds another layer of accomplishment.

It's part of the rhythm of the game, the cadence of the game. If we set past generations apart as special cases, we're really saying that today's baseball is the genuine article and all that went before was just preparation. Well, I don't buy that. Sure every generation feels that its heroes are the real McCoy, but we shouldn't ignore the legends of the past either, because our children

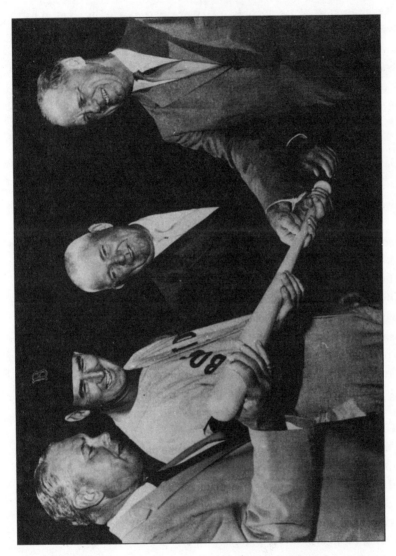

Terry, Williams, Hornsby and Sisler: four members of the elite .400 club.

NATIONAL BASEBALL LIBRARY AND ARCHIVE, COOPERSTOWN, N.Y.

and grandchildren would then find it just as easy to dismiss the baseball heroes of the '70s, '80s, and '90s . . . and on and on.

So while it isn't easy to compare the Cobbs and Jacksons with the Schmidts and Aarons, my Hit List is a ranking of the greatest hitters of all time with no special conditions attached. And no apologies.

I do regret that I didn't have a chance to observe some of the great players from before the turn of the century. Honus Wagner is the only hitter in this book whose career began before 1900. This is certainly not a comment on the calibre of 19th century baseball. Hitters like Nap Lajoie, Sam Crawford, Dan Brouthers, Cap Anson and Sam Thompson would doubtlessly excel in any era. I'll leave it to the true baseball scholars to more thoroughly sing their praises.

There's one other shamefully glaring historical fact that had a basic and profound influence on the makeup of my list. Until Jackie Robinson took the field for the Brooklyn Dodgers in 1947, blacks were denied the opportunity to show what they could do at the major league level. It's impossible to project what a hitter like Josh Gibson would have done against major league pitching, but based on eyewitness reports he was something to see. Who will ever know how many potential Aarons never got to show their stuff in the big leagues? As I said in my Hall of Fame induction speech, Gibson and other Negro League stars were robbed of that chance. I'm sure our list would look a bit different if the color barrier had never existed. Sadly we'll never know, and baseball is all the poorer because of it.

Having said that, it is appropriate and important to point out the watershed events that had a significant influence on the very nature of the game over the years and, by doing that, to put things in some basic historical context.

In the 1954 edition of *Baseball Stars* magazine, I discussed the practical differences between players of different eras in an article called "How to hit .400." In the time of Hornsby, Cobb, and Terry, I argued, there was no night ball, no twilight-night doubleheaders, no one night stands and one day hops. The players of those days had a regular daily schedule. All his games began at 3:30 p.m. He was able to eat breakfast in the morning, lunch at noon and dinner at night. He didn't have to worry about playing under the hot sun one day and in damp heavy night air the next. When the game was over he could expect a normal period of relaxation and plenty of rest that night. It's not surprising that Nap Lajoie hit .426 in 1901; Joe Jackson hit .408 in 1911; Ty Cobb hit .420 in 1911, .410 in 1912 and .401 in 1922; George Sisler hit .407 in 1920 and .420 in 1922; Harry Heilmann hit .403

in 1923; Rogers Hornsby hit .401 in 1922, .424 in 1924, and .403 in 1925; Bill Terry hit .401 in 1930.

As I went on to point out, It was the era of the dead ball, but it was a quick dead ball. Maybe it didn't go over the fence but it kept dropping over the infield for base hits. In 1911 Ty Cobb collected 248 hits but only eight went the distance. Frank "Home Run" Baker led the league with nine homers. In fact, the entire American league collected only 193 homers, less than the Brooklyn Dodgers racked up in 1953. The lively ball no doubt increases the home run output but it is no boon to the batting average. The best proof is that in the very same year, 1911, the National League, for the first time, tried the livelier cork center ball, while the American League stuck to the standard "dead" one. Honus Wagner, the N.L.'s leading hitter, batted .344 to Cobb's .420, while the N.L. hit 314 homers.

I sounded almost envious when I talked about those good old days, especially that notorious year of 1930:

1930 was a great year for batters. Bill Terry hit .401. Thirteen National Leaguers and nine American Leaguers batted over .350. 93 players in both leagues hit over .300. Those fellows were not "natural hitters," they were dedicated students of the art of hitting. They practiced hitting before and after the game. They knew all about the different woods. They knew as much or more about opposing pitchers than their managers. They became students of meteorology. They studied the winds and the air currents. They made a study of pitching mounds in every ball park. They spent hours watching the pitchers for telltale signs, what they threw, how they threw, whether they tipped their pitches. They lived and dreamed baseball. That was their way of life.

I went on to contrast the "simplicity" of the dead ball era with problems hitters of the fast-paced '50s faced in their quest for the magic .400:

Suppose it's Sunday. You play a doubleheader in New York, rest awhile and have dinner at 8. You find you have to play the next day under the lights in Boston so you get on a sleeper, breakfast on the train and eat dinner at the hotel between 3 and 4 o'clock in the afternoon. You're at the ballpark by 6, loggy after the meal, but you feel better at 8 when the game begins, though the air is damp and heavy, there's dew on the grass, and a chill wind comes up. The game ends at 11, you grab a sandwich, and hit the hay at 2 a.m. Between 10 and 11 next morning you arise just in time to have breakfast and dash out to the park for a game which starts maybe at 1:30, or maybe as late as 3. No wonder a really great hitter like Joe DiMaggio never cracked the exclusive .400 circle.

Boy, the more things change the more they remain the same. I'm sure Ty Cobb and Harry Heilmann were complaining about how easy it was for Honus Wagner and Hugh Duffy and all the guys who came before them too. It's almost laughable. Sure the game has progressed and society has changed, training methods are superior and all of that, but in the end I think it all evens out. There were pressures in the dead ball era, there were different pressures when I played, and today's players face a whole new set of problems and pressures. Some things have been made a lot easier for them and some are probably tougher too. In the end, though, a hitter still has to prove himself at the plate, and a truly great hitter would stand out in any era. You can just bet a smart guy like Tyrus Raymond Cobb would be able to make adjustments to his swing and terrorize the pitchers of 1996, just as he did those poor sods back in his own era.

Baseball's Generation Gap
A Brief History

Nonetheless, it's important to be aware of some of the milestones in the chronology of baseball and how they affected hitting:

- From the turn of the century to 1910, the baseball, featuring a rubber center, can best be described as dead.

- In the 1910 World Series, a cushioned cork center was introduced, enlivening the ball. In 1911 American League averages soared 30 points over the previous year; Ty Cobb batted .420. The NL homer king stroked 21, compared to 10 for the previous year's winner.

- In 1920 the ball was dramatically enlivened. .400 seasons became commonplace and home run totals soared. Ruth had 11 homers in 1918, 29 in 1919, 54 in 1920, and 59 in 1921.

- In 1930 the baseball was once again juiced up, this time for one season only. It still allowed ample time for Hack Wilson to stroke 56 homers and drive in a record 190 runs before becoming a mere mortal the following year with 13 HRs and 61 RBIs. Bill Terry hit .401 in 1930. He was the last National Leaguer to reach that mark, but three other senior circuit batters hit better than .380 that year, and the overall league batting average was a lofty .303.

- Over the years there have been a number of other developments which have produced varying and perhaps cumulative effects on hitting. Night baseball (1935), domed stadiums (1965), artificial turf (1966), lowering the pitcher's mound (1969), changing the strike zone (1969), expansion of the major leagues (1961, '62, '68, '77, etc.), and the advent of air travel have all had an impact. These represent the natural growing pains of the sport, however, and have altered the fundamental nature of the battle between pitcher and batter very little.

The Philly Factor

There's another factor that plays a role in the creation of the great hitter, and it has nothing to do with on-field performance: the media. Players who perform in the spotlight in New York or Los Angeles tend to get more attention and coverage than those in smaller cities like St. Louis or Atlanta — at least before Ted Turner and CNN turned that Georgia city into a media mecca. Hank Aaron in Milwaukee and Atlanta got much less ink than Willie Mays in New York and San Francisco for precisely that reason. Players like Frank Robinson would have been major stars if they had played in New York instead of Cincinnati and Baltimore.

Both Al Simmons and Chuck Klein, both members of my Hit List, are classic examples of this phenomenon. Both performed in Philadelphia, and their feats went largely unnoticed outside the Keystone State. W. C. Fields' headstone supposedly reads, "On the whole, I'd rather be in Philadelphia." For talented ballplayers of that era, the City of Brotherly Love constituted something of a media graveyard in comparison with larger centers.

THE HIT LIST

Statistically Speaking

I didn't want *Ted Williams' Hit List* to be a dry statistical analysis of what I think is the most exciting and uniquely human facet of baseball, but I did want to be able to back up my insights with some hard and fast truths. The statistical categories employed in this book and on the chart on page 56 represent traditional yardsticks of excellence such as batting averages, home run and RBI totals, slugging percentage, on base percentage — and production, one of the newer statistics developed to allow for a more fair and complete standard of hitting excellence. Here is a brief glossary of statistical terms.

On base percentage, a statistic developed in the early '50s, was refined and adopted by major league baseball in 1984. Following the lead of Thorn and Palmer in *Total Baseball*, I have omitted sacrifice flies from the equation for purposes of greater accuracy. On base percentage (OBP) is obtained by calculating hits plus walks plus hit by pitch and then dividing by at-bats plus walks plus hit by pitch.

Slugging percentage is arrived at by dividing total bases by at-bats. A home run, for example, represents four bases, a triple three, and so on.

Rank	Hitter/Bats	At-Bats	Batting Avg.	Slugging Pct.	On Base Pct.
1	Ruth B:L	8399	.342	.690	.474
2	Gehrig B:L	8001	.340	.632	.447
3	Foxx B:R	8134	.325	.609	.428
4	Hornsby B:R	8173	.358	.577	.434
5	DiMaggio B:R	8821	.325	.579	.398
6	Cobb B:L	11,434	.366	.512	.432
7	Musial B:L	10,972	.331	.559	.418
8	Jackson B:L	4981	.356	.517	.423
9	Aaron B:R	12,364	.305	.555	.377
10	Mays B:R	10,881	.302	.557	.387
11	Greenberg B:R	5193	.313	.605	.412
12	Mantle B:R&L	8102	.298	.557	.423
13	Speaker B:L	10,208	.345	.500	.424
14	Simmons B:R	8759	.334	.535	.380
15	Mize B:L	6443	.312	.562	.397
16	Ott B:L	9456	.304	.533	.414
17	Heilmann B:R	7787	.342	.520	.410
18	Robinson B:R	10,006	.294	.537	.392
19	Schmidt B:R	8352	.267	.527	.384
20	Kiner B:R	5205	.279	.548	.398
21	Snider B:L	7161	.295	.540	.381
22	Killebrew B:R	8147	.256	.509	.379
23	McCovery B:L	8197	.270	.515	.377
24	Klein B:L	6486	.320	.543	.379
25	J. Gibson B:R	No Stats Available			
/	Williams B:L	7706	.344	.634	.483

Home Runs	At-Bats Per H.R.	At-Bats Per Strike Out	Runs Batted In	At-Bats Per RBI	Prod-uction
714	11.76	6.32	2209	3.80	1.163
493	16.23	10.14	1990	4.02	1.080
534	15.23	6.20	1922	4.23	1.038
301	27.15	12.04	1584	5.16	1.010
361	18.89	18.49	1537	4.44	.977
118	97.73	21.06	1933	5.90	.945
475	23.10	15.76	1951	5.62	.977
54	92.24	26.48	785	6.35	.940
755	16.38	8.94	2297	5.38	.932
660	16.49	7.13	1903	5.72	.944
331	15.69	6.15	1276	4.07	1.017
536	15.12	4.74	1509	5.37	.979
117	87.24	46.40	1559	6.54	.924
307	28.53	11.88	1827	4.79	.915
359	17.95	12.30	1337	4.82	.959
.511	18.50	10.55	1860	5.08	.947
183	42.55	14.16	1538	5.06	.930
586	17.08	6.53	1812	5.52	.929
548	15.24	4.44	1595	5.24	.911
369	14.11	6.95	1015	5.13	.946
407	17.59	5.79	1333	5.37	.921
573	14.22	4.80	1584	5.14	.887
521	15.73	5.29	1555	5.27	.892
300	21.62	12.45	1201	5.40	.922
521	14.79	10.87	1839	4.19	1.116

Production is the sum of on base percentage and slugging percentage. *Total Baseball* describes it as "a simple but elegant measure of batting prowess, in that the weaknesses of one-half of the formulation, On Base Percentage, are countered by the strengths of the other, Slugging Average, and vice versa." As I pointed out earlier, I have chosen not to use the PRO./A (production/adjusted) refinement that mathematically factors in home park dimensions and league averages. I have decided instead to let my knowledge of these and other factors be my guide.

1

George Herman (Babe) Ruth

Career: 1914-1935

Bats: L **Height: 6'2"** **Weight: 215**

His record says it all. Babe Ruth is the greatest hitter to ever play this game and the most famous athlete who ever lived. I was tempted to refer to his real-life exploits as Bunyanesque, but you could just as easily call Paul Bunyan's feats Ruthian. Now *that* tells you something about the man: when you talk about those two American legends the terms are practically interchangeable. The difference is that Bunyan was a fictional character while Ruth actually *did* those things, and while fact and fiction may become a bit blurry when people talk about the Bambino, the cold hard facts are enough to place him in a league by himself.

No wonder America loved Ruth. He did more for baseball than probably any other individual. He was easily baseball's most significant figure. He brought it back after the Black Sox gambling scandal, and he rejuvenated the game. He was a tremendous drawing card, a charismatic type of individual who was just perfect for the job. The game of baseball pretty near catered to what he could do. They livened up the ball. They built Yankee Stadium because of him. They did everything.

Who's to say he wasn't the greatest? I don't know. Cripes, he was certainly the greatest power hitter this game ever saw, bar none. They say he borrowed his swing from Shoeless Joe Jackson. Wherever he got it, he went on an offensive rampage that will never be touched. He couldn't run that well — he looked more like a sumo wrestler than a ballplayer — but he still hit .342 lifetime. He owns the major league record for the highest slugging percentage in a season, with .847 in 1920 .847! He "dropped" to .846 the next year. His 714 lifetime homers stood as the all-time record until Aaron broke it in 1973. He hit 50 homers four times and 40 or more 11 times. His total of 60 round-trippers remains the record for a 154-game schedule.

EXCLUSIVE — COPYRIGHTED PHOTO
GEORGE LYONS
E ONLY PICTURE EVER TAKEN IN UNIFORM
FIRST MEETING OF

I personally think that Babe Ruth has to be the greatest player of all time.

GEORGE LYONS

The very fact that Ruth hit so many more home runs per time at bat than other hitters puts him in a class by himself. A home run every 12 times up is almost unbelievable. Ruth led the American League in homers 12 times, and he holds a *lifetime* slugging percentage of .690, the best by far.

I personally think that Ruth *has* to be the greatest player of all time, and I'll tell you why I think that. He was not only a great slugger — the greatest slugger the game has ever seen or ever will see — but also a great pitcher. I know we're talking about hitters here, but you can't ignore the fact that he was one of the best pitchers of his time. He compiled a 94-46 win-loss record with a skimpy 2.28 ERA. They'll never make me believe that he was a great outfielder, but all the old-timers will tell you that he did a good job: never threw to the wrong base and all that stuff. And he played right field in Yankee Stadium, which is a tough field to play. More importantly, he resurrected the game with his allure for the fans and his flamboyant style of play. And his hitting! I'm damn sure the fans didn't come to see Ruth play right field, they came to see him hit. And he never disappointed them.

He had such magnetism about him, and he was the guy with all the slugging marks. Ruth dwarfed everybody during his day, and the great players of the time all looked in awe to him. These were Ruth's contemporaries, guys who had fought tooth and nail to beat his hated Yankees, and still he was the man they all looked up to as the draw, as the game itself — or at least as the savior of the game. Eddie Collins was a great player himself — a Hall of Famer — but when he talked about Ruth he talked about him with reverence. Looking back, it's not much of an exaggeration to say that Ruth saved the game of baseball. When the Black Sox scandal threatened to destroy the integrity of the game, it was Ruth who led the national pastime out of its darkest hour and into a new era of popularity. He had those gaudy statistics, and he was an outrageous kind of guy. He had a zest for life and a kind of roguish charm that captured the imagination of the American public. Hell, he changed the very nature of the game by moving the focus from finesse to power. You know, they call it a game of inches — and it certainly was for his contemporaries — but it was usually transformed into a game of 500-600 feet when Ruth came to bat.

During the so-called dead ball era, he hit more homers than anyone ever before. Then when the ball was enlivened in 1920, he exploded for 54 round-trippers, more than any single American League team.

I read a book in which Ruth talked about hitting, and he said it pretty near the way I would say it. He described it a little differently, just like some of these guys today are saying things differently than I did in *The Science of*

Hitting, but he certainly indicated that you had to have a good ball to hit and all the rest. What he said I liked and I agreed with.

I only met Ruth once, at an old-timers event in 1944 when he was close to 50 years old. It was an exhibition game for some charity. I watched him closely and even hten he still had that fluidity to his swing. But he had gotten pretty fat by then, and I remember that he hurt his back that day swinging the bat. It must have been 106 degrees in the shade, and he and some other old-timers were drinking beer throughout the game.

Even today the name Ruth is synonymous with baseball and, especially, with hitting. He played his last major league game more than 60 years ago and you can still hear kids in school yards taunting their friends with, "Who do you think you are, Babe Ruth?" Hell, his name is as well-known now as it was when he played. You can't say that about any other American athlete.

Appropriately, Babe Ruth hit the very first All-Star game home run. It was a two-run shot at Comiskey Park in Chicago in July of 1933. Babe's American Leaguers won 4-2 over the National League's best.

Ballpark Figures: Yankee Stadium, "The House that Ruth Built." Left field was 280.58' in 1923, and 301' in 1928. Deep left center was 460' in '23. Centerfield was 490' in '23. Deep right center was 429' in '23. Right field was 294.75' in 1923, and 295' in 1930.

Lifetime Stats

Years Played: 22	**Runs Batted In:** 2209
Games: 2503	**Bases on Balls:** 2056
At-bats: 8399	**Strikeouts:** 1330
Runs: 2174	**Batting Average:** .342
Hits: 2873	**On Base Percentage:** .474
Doubles: 506	**Slugging Percentage:** .690
Triples: 136	**Production:** 1.163
Home Runs: 714	

2

Lou Gehrig

Career: 1923-1939

Bats: L   **Height: 6'1"**   **Weight: 212**

Babe Ruth epitomized the power and the glory of the Yankee dynasties, DiMaggio represented Yankee style and class, and my friend Mickey Mantle exemplified rawboned Yankee talent. It took Lou Gehrig to put all those things together in one package. That's why he will forever remain the Pride of the Yankees. To me it's much more than just a catchy Hollywood title.

The courage that Gehrig showed in facing the disease that bears his name, and that eventually took his life, is the stuff of legend, but long before that he proved that he was something special — a man of iron. He played in 2130 consecutive games from June 1, 1925, to April 30, 1939, before finally asking to be taken out. Until that fateful day arrived, he went head to head with teammate Babe Ruth, and not only held his own but in some phases of the game even managed to surpass the Babe.

You look at Babe Ruth and you look at Lou Gehrig and you say to yourself, "Hell, there's no difference between the two. They're about the same." And they were! How in the world a team could have a one-two punch like that, I'll be a dirty son of a gun if I know — although some guys have come close for a season, maybe. In recent years the Oakland A's came pretty close with their two big guns, Canseco (now with the Red Sox) and McGwire. They are not as good hitters, of course, but they're tough hitters, big strong guys who had a lot of other guys around them who could wear you out. In the early '60s Mantle and Maris also did it for a year or two. But Ruth and Gehrig did it throughout their careers. That's the difference.

In 1927 Gehrig hit 47 homers and was still outdone by Ruth, who picked that year to hit 60. Still, with the exception of Ruth, I don't think any player could have matched Lou Gehrig if Gehrig could have played out his career in good health. Only God knows what he'd have done. His statistics

I don't think any player could match Lou Gehrig if Gehrig could have played out his career in good health. NATIONAL BASEBALL LIBRARY & ARCHIVE, COOPERSTOWN, N.Y.

are so close to Ruth's in every way, and still he was up barely 8000 times (8001 official at-bats). Some of these guys are up 13,000 times and still haven't managed as many home runs as Gehrig.

When you think of Ruth, you automatically think of Gehrig. And vice-versa. How the heck can you separate those two guys? They were both .340 hitters. They both slugged well over .600. Gehrig didn't loft the ball as much as Ruth but he sure as hell hit it hard. He hit screaming liners. And he was a faster runner than Ruth. He stole home 15 times in his career, and I can't picture Ruth doing that.

Gehrig was the son of German immigrants who knew about the importance of education. He attended Columbia University on a football and baseball scholarship, and I'll tell you, there weren't very many college guys in the game at that time. He graduated to the Yankees in 1923, and his 17-year career stands as a monument to consistency. He led the American League in home runs three times (one tie), in RBIs five times (one tie), and in batting average once.

A two-time MVP, he set the American League record in 1931 for most RBIs with 184, a total that even the Babe couldn't match. In 1934 he captured the Triple Crown with a .363 average, 49 homers, and 165 RBIs.

Gehrig's lifetime grand-slam total is really incredible. He came through in those clutch situations a record 23 times. For 13 straight years he drove in more than 100 runs and averaged 147 RBIs during that span. He once hit four homers in one game, and for 12 consecutive seasons he blasted more than 20 home runs per season, averaging 38. That's a barrage! No wonder they called him the Iron Horse.

In the 1932 World Series he led the charge with a .529 average, three homers and eight RBIs in a four-game Yankee sweep of the Chicago Cubs. He did all that damage in only 17 trips to the plate.

In 1938 Gehrig's statistics started to wane just a bit. His batting average dipped below .300 for the first time since his first full season, and he hit "only" 29 home runs and drove in 114. People thought he had a bit of an off year, but they sure didn't expect that it was the beginning of the end.

I still remember that one game that Gehrig played against me in 1939, his last year as a Yankee. I was a rookie with the Red Sox, and I remember he hit a humpbacked line drive to me his first time up and grounded out the next time. I seem to recall that he swung down on the ball a bit, but he still had amazing power. I remember following him up the stairs to the field a couple of times that day . . . a raw rookie following the great Lou Gehrig up the steps . . . and I remember thinking that he looked pretty good — not great, but pretty good even then. Of course, I didn't know what he was facing at the time. He quit just eight games later and was almost immediately named to the Hall of Fame.

On July 4th of that year 61,000 fans jammed into Yankee Stadium to pay tribute to Gehrig. He responded with that memorable speech in which he said, "Today I consider myself the luckiest man on the face of the earth."

Can you imagine what desperate thoughts must have gone through pitchers' minds when they had to face Ruth and Gehrig on a hot afternoon at Yankee Stadium? He was a great hitter. So great that he was able to play alongside the most flamboyant figure in the history of American sport and still emerge as a star in his own right.

The 1927 Yankees, featuring Babe Ruth and Lou Gehrig, is often called the "greatest team ever." Ruth hit a record 60 homers, led the American League in runs scored (158), bases on balls (138), on base percentage (.487), and slugging average (.772). But it was Gehrig, with 47 homers and a league-leading 52 doubles and 175 RBIs, who was chosen league MVP that year.

Ballpark Figures: During Gehrig's inspired career Yankee Stadium offered up the following targets for the left-handed slugger. Left field was 280.58' until 1928, when it expanded to 301'. Deep left center was 460' until 1937 when it became 457'. Centerfield was 490' in 1923 and shrank to 461' in '37. Right center moved from 429' in '23 to 407' in '37. Right field was 294.75' in '23 and 295' in 1930.

Lifetime Stats

Years Played: 17	**Runs Batted In:** 1990
Games: 2164	**Bases on Balls:** 1508
At-bats: 8001	**Strikeouts:** 789
Runs: 1888	**Batting Average:** .340
Hits: 2721	**On Base Percentage:** .447
Doubles: 534	**Slugging Percentage:** .632
Triples: 163	**Production:** 1.080
Home Runs: 493	

3

Jimmie Foxx

Career: 1925-1945

Bats: R   **Height: 5'11½"**   **Weight: 190**

If you asked the baseball gods to design the perfect power hitter, they would probably just point to Jimmie Foxx and say, "It's already been done." When you talk about power, you start with Foxx and Ruth. Foxx carried on where Ruth had left off. He inherited the long ball mantle that the Bambino had created. If anyone was ever capable of actually tearing the cover off the ball, it would be Double X, my teammate when I first came to the Red Sox. They also called him The Beast, but really he was just a big gentle Maryland farm boy with bulging biceps.

Now Jimmie Foxx may not have been the most intelligent hitter I ever knew, but he certainly wasn't a dumb guy: he was smart at working a pitcher. Hell, he knew just how they were going to pitch, and he'd just lay for it, and when Foxx got his pitch he hit it like Mantle.

It sounded like cherry bombs going off when Foxx hit them. Hank Greenberg hit them pretty near as far, but they didn't sound that same way. They sounded like firecrackers when Mantle and Foxx hit them — and I never heard anyone say that about Ruth's or Greenberg's home runs. Foxx and Mantle were two guys from different eras, but I saw quite a bit of them both. I never saw another right-handed hitter, except Mantle and Foxx, really crush the ball — I mean *crush* it — when he hit it like those guys did. Killebrew could hit them hard at times, but I don't think it made the same sound. No, it might make a crack, but I always thought that Mantle's and Jimmie Foxx's sounded just a little different. They were both built the same, and I've got to think that they both generated great bat speed.

I played three years with Foxx and he was toward the end of his career, but I do have to say that the year before I played with him he hit 50 home runs, and he led the league with 35 in my rookie year of 1939, so he wasn't

It sounded like cherry bombs when Foxx hit them.

NATIONAL BASEBALL LIBRARY & ARCHIVE, COOPERSTOWN, N.Y.

too shabby even when I arrived on the scene. We were on a road trip in '39 and I had a chance to see Jimmie Foxx's greatest performance as a hitter, and I'll always remember it.

He warmed up by hitting a humungous shot over the left-field bleachers in Chicago. Then we moved on to Cleveland. I was on second base and Mel Harder was pitching for Cleveland at Municipal Stadium, and he was really fooling everyone with his stuff. All day his pitches were either sailing or they were sinking. This was long before the Indians organization shortened the distances by installing those inner home run fences. Foxx hit a drive to left center over the 435-foot mark that went over the wall into the seats way, way back there. I mean, he hit it a ton. It must have carried close to 500 feet in the air.

After that we went to Detroit, and he hit one into the upper deck in the left centerfield bleachers, a mile back there. It was the longest ball I'd ever seen hit. So I saw Jimmie hit three long home runs in three series in three different cities toward the end of his career. And I'll never, ever forget those home run blasts.

Back at Fenway I remember him hitting this long, long homer over the Wall into the teeth of a gale, and I remember looking at all those muscles as he trotted around the bases, and shaking that huge hand of his as he crossed the plate, and feeling almost weak. I was a skinny little guy anyway, and I felt weak in comparison to Jimmie Foxx.

For 12 seasons, from 1929 to 1940, Jimmie never hit less than 30 homers a season, and he *averaged* 40 homers during that period. He rang up 13 consecutive 100-plus-RBI seasons and maintained a career batting average of .325. That's a combination of power and average that is almost unheard of among modern-day hitters. Today they are either power hitters or hitters for average, but they are very seldom both.

Oh, Foxx was a hell of a player — and he was a very popular guy. He was a big old lovable bear of a guy. He could run pretty near as fast as Mantle, and he was built the same way. On the Red Sox we used to say, "Look at that son of a gun run." He would always talk about what he'd look for next time up. He'd say, "He'll give us that cheap curve," or, "I know he's going to bust me high and tight all the time." No detailed technical theories on the science of hitting, just a wealth of practical advice gained from years of experience. He was obviously good at reading the pitchers. Joe Cronin used to get me together with veterans like Foxx, Joe Vosmik, and Doc Cramer to talk hitting on those long train trips. Cronin realized that this would help to shake things up and get a young player like myself revved up. For an impressionable young hitter like myself, just being in the presence of a wily old veteran like Foxx was better than an all-day hitting clinic. It was like a tonic.

If production is the yardstick of the great hitter — and I sincerely believe that it is — then Jimmie Foxx must be the Henry Ford of hitters. Hell, he had production numbers that would have made Lee Iacocca envious.

Pitching ace Lefty Gomez once faced Jimmie Foxx in a key situation at Yankee Stadium. Time after time Lefty continued to shake off catcher Bill Dickey's signs. Finally the exasperated Dickey made a trip to the mound and demanded to know just what pitch the future Hall of Famer wanted to throw. "Nothing," replied Gomez. "I figure if I wait a while, maybe he'll get a phone call."

Ballpark Figures: Foxx spent his career in Philadelphia's Shibe Park and Boston's Fenway Park. Shibe Park, where Foxx toiled from 1925 to 1935, offered the following test for the right-handed power hitter. Left field was 334' in 1922, changed to 312' in '26, and to 334' in '30. Left center was 387' in 1922, and moved back to 405' in '25. Centerfield was 468'. Right center was 393'. Foxx's second home (1936-42), venerable, angular old Fenway, featured a 37' wall known as the Green Monster just 315' away in left field. Left center was 379' beginning in 1934, and deep left center extended to 388'. Centerfield was 468' in 1930, and 388.67' in '34. The deepest corner, just to the right of dead center, was 420' in 1934. Right field was 332' in 1936, 322' in '38, 332' in '39, 304' in '40, and 302' in '42.

Lifetime Stats

Years Played: 20	**Runs Batted In:** 1922
Games: 2317	**Bases on Balls:** 1452
At-bats: 8134	**Strikeouts:** 1311
Runs: 1751	**Batting Average:** .325
Hits: 2646	**On Base Percentage:** .428
Doubles: 458	**Slugging Percentage:** .609
Triples: 125	**Production:** 1.038
Home Runs: 534	

4

Rogers Hornsby

Career: 1915-1937

Bats: R   **Height: 5'11½"**   **Weight: 200**

Rogers Hornsby can lay legitimate claim to being one of the greatest right-handed hitters of all time. They called him the "Rajah," and his career began in the dead ball era, but it really sprang to life, along with the ball, in the 1920s. He came very close to being the perfect hitter, if such a creature exists.

Starting in 1921 he averaged an incredible .402 over a five-year span, and in 1924 he achieved the highest average in the modern history of the game, hitting .424. His .358 lifetime mark is second only to Ty Cobb's .367, but unlike Cobb over in the American League, Hornsby also featured power in his offensive arsenal. In fact, he led the National League in homers on two separate occasions and hit over 300 round-trippers throughout his career. What a combination of power and average!

Hornsby was one of my coaches at the Red Sox farm team in Minneapolis when I first came up. He was one of the most knowledgeable guys I have ever talked hitting with. Here I was, a 19-year-old kid, and he wanted to talk about hitting all the time. Boy, I sure took advantage of the opportunity to pick his brains. And Hornsby was a smart hitter too. He gave me the most positive advice when I asked him, "What do I have to do to become a great hitter?" He couldn't have been nicer, and I'll always have a warm spot in my heart for him. Hornsby's advice was this: "Get a good ball to hit." That was it! He said you've got to get a good ball to hit. So that wasn't even my golden rule (as espoused in *The Science of Hitting*)— it was his.

Actually, I'd already had that rule but without knowing how important it was. I walked a hundred times in the Pacific Coast League at 18 years of

Hornsby came very close to being the perfect hitter — if such a creature exists.

NATIONAL BASEBALL LIBRARY & ARCHIVE, COOPERSTOWN, N.Y.

age, and I walked 150 times in Minneapolis at 19, so you know I instinctively got a good ball to hit. Then I got a little stronger, kept getting a little better, and all of a sudden I was cranking them a little better. Now they were a little more afraid of me and BOOM, BOOM, BOOM. Hell, I was a young, skinny, 155-lb kid at 6'3", but as I got stronger and I got better and I got more experience — BOOM — it all fell together. When I got to the majors, I realized that was the best advice Hornsby ever gave me. It gave me a foundation for my hitting career.

Hornsby used to stay after practice almost every day while I hit. He was over 40 at the time but he was still as keen as mustard. You have to think that all that time I spent around him had an impact on me. We used to have little contests — line drive hitting contests — and I'll tell you he could still sting them even then.

I looked up Hornsby and you can look him up too. I said to myself, you know, Hornsby hit all the time in St. Louis. He was a right-center hitter, and right center in the Brown's ballpark (Sportsman's Park) was 365 feet away. It was a cozy ballpark for him. That's where Musial hit too, but Hornsby — whew — just hit them out there. He could hit them all over, but he was a right centerfield hitter to a great degree and the park really helped him. And he could run like a deer.

Now in addition to all these pluses, the ground is harder than rock in St. Louis, so the balls went through right field like a rocket. So I said, "Goddamn, no wonder he hit so good!" Well, he got in trouble with principal owner Sam Breadon of the Cardinals and they traded him to the New York Giants. He had just gotten through hitting .424, .403, and .317 in St. Louis and they traded him to New York (in 1927) with those Death Valleys in right center and left center. You know, he hit .361 that year, so he could hit anywhere! You can't deny his accomplishments by pointing to the cozy dimensions of his ballparks in places like St. Louis and Chicago. The record book shows that he hit .359 at home during his career and .358 on the road. That should close the book on that subject.

Hornsby captured six consecutive National League batting championships (seven in all) and led the senior circuit in slugging percentage ten times. In 19 of his 23 major league seasons he batted .300 or better.

In 1937, he cracked a dramatic pinch-hit homer to right field at Fenway — way, way back there in the deepest part of the ballpark. They were still talking about it five years after I came up to Boston.

Hornsby had an abrasive nature, and he was always criticizing DiMaggio — and he even got to criticizing me about what he saw as my refusal to hit to left field to foil the Lou Boudreau shift. He wanted to know who DiMaggio thought he was when he was asking for $27,000 a year in just his third year in the majors. Joe had just got through hitting 46 home runs with 167 runs batted in, and had batted .346, and Hornsby wanted to know who the hell this guy thought he was! Well, the greatest player I saw, that's who he was. After seeing up close what DiMaggio could do with his bat and his glove over the years, I made up my mind right there and then that I would never criticize a young player like that, because you just never know what they might end up doing. I almost did it with Mantle, but thankfully I didn't say it out loud.

So Hornsby wasn't overly diplomatic, and DiMaggio didn't like him, but Hornsby treated me as well as anybody could have treated me.

There are some similarities in our two careers. Hornsby and I remain the only two-time Triple Crown winners and we both came within a hair of winning three. He had great eyesight, and they always said that of me — although as I've said elsewhere in this book, my eyesight wasn't that good. And I guess you could say that we were both quite well respected and highly regarded by members of the umpiring fraternity because we very seldom questioned a call. I've read that Hornsby was so completely dedicated to hitting that he avoided movies and reading for fear that they would detract from his sharp eye at the plate. Hell, even I didn't go that far. It's funny because I like to think that a lot of young hitters have benefited from advice that Hornsby gave me and that I passed along in *The Science of Hitting*. Hornsby's advice would probably have been to save your eyes by not reading the book!

When Stan Musial was a household name in the '50s, former Cardinal owner Sam Breadon, the same guy who had feuded with Hornsby and eventually traded him to New York, was asked if Musial was his greatest player ever. They say Breadon thought it over and replied, "No, I couldn't say that. There was Hornsby." That shows you how great the Rajah was.

Rogers Hornsby's keen batting eye was respected throughout base-ball. Once, after three consecutive called balls to the Rajah, a brash young pitcher complained loudly to the umpire, only to watch as his fourth delivery landed in the distant bleachers. Hall of Fame arbiter Bill Klem patiently explained these events to the irate rookie. "When the ball is over the plate, young man, Mr. Hornsby will let you know."

Ballpark Figures: Sportsman's Park was home to the right-handed Rajah for much of his major league career. Left field was reduced from 350' to 340' in 1921, was changed to 355' in '26, 360' in '30, and 351.1' in '31. Left center was 379'. Centerfield was 430' in 1926. Right field was 325', changed to 315' in 1921 and 310' in '31.

Lifetime Stats

Years Played: 23
Games: 2259
At-bats: 8173
Runs: 1579
Hits: 2930
Doubles: 541
Triples: 169
Home Runs: 301

Runs Batted In: 1584
Bases on Balls: 1038
Strikeouts: 679
Batting Average: .358
On Base Percentage: .434
Slugging Percentage: .577
Production: 1.010

I idolized Joe DiMaggio.

NATIONAL BASEBALL LIBRARY & ARCHIVE, COOPERSTOWN, N.Y.

5

Joe DiMaggio

Career: 1936-1951

Bats: R   **Height: 6'2"**   **Weight: 193**

DiMaggio was the greatest all-round player I saw. I give it to him over Mays simply because he was a better hitter than Mays. I saw him play, I saw what he could do, and I'm positive that he was a better hitter than Mays. He didn't have quite the power that Willie had, but he was certainly smoother, and he was a classic hitter. DiMaggio was a .325 hitter despite playing half his games at a tough ballpark like Yankee Stadium, and he looked great doing it. At the plate he was poetry in motion; his fluid swing was a thing of beauty.

I can't say enough about DiMaggio. Of all the great major leaguers I played with or against during my 19-year career, he was my idol. I idolized Joe DiMaggio! The incredible thing about him is that his road record was even better than his home record at Yankee Stadium. Now, I had more home runs on the road than at Fenway, but DiMaggio was a better all-round hitter away from home. It just shows what a hell of a hitter he was. Still, in 13 seasons in New York he hit 148 homers in the Stadium, which is about 11 per season. He also owns the best home run to strikeout ratio in the history of the game, with 361 homers and only 369 strikeouts. That's a 1:1.02 ratio.

They were always making comparisons between DiMaggio and me. The sports pages were full of it in the '40s and early '50s. It was a hotly debated rivalry, and the media tried to find feuds where there was only mutual respect. The consensus seemed to be that I was the better hitter, but that DiMaggio was the consummate ballplayer. I sure had no argument with that verdict. For me, hitting was always my first consideration. Everyone asks what Joe would've done in Fenway. Armchair managers dreamed of a trade between the Yankees and Red Sox. It was a switch that was supposed to help both Joe and myself, and our respective clubs. On paper I suppose it looked like a deal made in Heaven, and legend has it that it was briefly agreed to by

Tom Yawkey and the Yankee brass one night. Both parties apparently thought better of it in the sober light of day.

Well, I'll tell you, I'd rather have seen DiMaggio in Detroit or even the Cleveland ballpark to break a record, because he could hit a ball well to centerfield and left center, but he could also hit a ball pretty well to right center. A good hitter can make accommodations to any ballpark, and that's what DiMaggio did, but he was not as good a hitter in New York as he'd have been in Detroit.

Basically Joe was a left-center, left-field hitter. We should have pulled shifts on him like they pulled on me, because he was a dead-pull hitter, and if he ever got one to the right of the shortstop. . . . Very few times have I seen him thrown out on a ball to the right of shortstop. He'd beat it out. That's how good he was going down the line. We never did throw him out.

Remember, I didn't say DiMaggio in Fenway, did I? Because that's a short porch, and he would have had a hell of a time getting a good pitch to hit. "The hell with him!" the pitchers would say, and they'd pitch him low and outside, low and outside — and all of a sudden he'd be hitting to no-man's land in centerfield. As a hitter, he'd be betwixt and between. He could pull the ball with anyone who ever played, but he'd have had it tough in Fenway because opposing pitchers wouldn't give him anything to pull. And against the Green Monster (Fenway Park's 37' left-field wall), he might not have hit so many home runs anyway, because DiMaggio was not a lofty-type hitter. He could hit the ball high, but it generally wasn't the Greenberg type of homer; it was the Foxx kind of homer, more BOOM, BOOM, more like hard, high line drive homers. The Wall might have turned some of those shots into long singles. So I think DiMaggio would have fared better in Detroit, and I think he'd have fared well in Cleveland at Municipal Stadium.

DiMaggio was a stylish hitter, the most stylish right-handed hitter I ever saw. And even if he didn't hit it well, he had a chance to beat it out. Against Joe, the infield was always playing back, and he got a chance to beat it out, because for a right-handed hitter he got away from the plate really well.

It's incredible to think that during DiMaggio's 56-game hitting streak in 1941 he never attempted a single bunt in 223 official at-bats. During that streak he batted at a .408 clip and showed some power with 16 doubles, 4 triples, and 15 homers. He won the MVP that year, although some people felt that I should have gotten it, because I hit .406 that same season. Well, I never felt I should have won it in '41! DiMaggio had an incredible year and led the Yankees to the pennant. There's no doubt that his streak was one of the most amazing feats in baseball history.

Joe captured the American League MVP award three times in all, in 1939, '41, and '47. He led our league in homers twice, in RBIs twice and in batting average twice. He finished his career with 361 homers, a .325 batting average, and 1537 RBIs. He was named to the Hall of Fame in 1955.

There's no question that the two premier hitters in the American League for 15 years were DiMaggio and myself. But no one has greater admiration for DiMaggio as a hitter than Ted Williams. Joe DiMaggio could do it all. He hit the ball hard! Screeching line drives. He was smart and he was good. I was almost inclined to put him ahead of Hornsby as a great right-handed hitter, but you can't deny Hornsby's stats.

But Joe DiMaggio's career cannot be summed up in numbers and awards. It might sound corny, but he had a profound and lasting impact on the country. How many athletes can make that claim? Despite what Simon and Garfunkel sang about him, every baseball fan knows that DiMaggio could never really leave us. For many fans he's become baseball's knight in shining pinstripe armor. Hell, for some he was almost the embodiment of the American dream. In fact when that earthquake hit San Francisco during the World Series a few years ago, the commentators made references to DiMaggio's home as if it were the residence of royalty.

As far as I'm concerned, they weren't far wrong.

Marilyn Monroe, otherwise known as Mrs. Joe DiMaggio, returned from entertaining the troops in Korea with stories of the warm reception she had been accorded from 100,000 lonely soldiers. "Joe," she gushed breathlessly, "you've never heard such cheering!" "Yes, I have," the Yankee Clipper gently replied.

Ballpark Figures: The right-handed DiMaggio played his entire career in New York's Yankee Stadium, a ballpark which seems much better suited to left-handed pull hitters. Left field measured 301' down the line, falling away to 402', 415', and 457' in deep left center; then to 466' at the left of centerfield screen, 461' in centerfield, 407' in right center; and 295' to 296' in right field.

Lifetime Stats

Years Played: 13
Games: 1736
At-bats: 6821
Runs: 1390
Hits: 2214
Doubles: 389
Triples: 131
Home Runs: 361

Runs Batted In: 1537
Bases on Balls: 790
Strikeouts: 369
Batting Average: .325
On Base Percentage: .398
Slugging Percentage: .579
Production: .977

6

Ty Cobb

Career: 1905-1928

Bats: L   **Height: 6'1"**   **Weight: 175**

Ty Cobb was a man possessed of keen intelligence, blazing speed and unsurpassed batting skills. And I guess some would say that he sometimes played the game like a man possessed. Period. With all that he accomplished he should have been the quintessential American hero. Instead he is seen as baseball's eternal antihero. He had an all-consuming passion for perfection, and while it drove him to greatness on the field, it also helped to alienate him from teammates, opponents, and fans.

Cobb was the one and only. He was the greatest all-round player of his generation, and some of the old-timers will tell you he was the best of all time. He was certainly in the same league as Ruth for his contribution to baseball. There's no denying his greatness. Cobb hit .366 lifetime — the highest in the history of baseball — and no one will ever do it again. He was revered by his opponents. Even his severest critics had the greatest reverence and admiration for his talent. I think of all the players who ever lived — every player who ever lived — Tyrus Raymond Cobb was the fiercest competitor who ever walked on a baseball field.

I didn't actually see him play, but he was so intelligent, and at 6'1" and 175 lbs he was big for his day. And he was fast as lightning stealing bases. Put it all together: total bases, .366 average, sliding this way, sliding that way, stealing home! He did everything, so you know you had to respect Tyrus Raymond.

The Georgia Peach reached the coveted .400 mark on three separate occasions and captured a record 10 American League batting crowns. In 23 of his 24 seasons he batted .300 or better. Many of his batting and base-running feats will never be equaled. He stole home an incredible 35 times,

Tyrus Raymond Cobb was the fiercest competitor who ever walked onto a baseball field. NATIONAL BASEBALL LIBRARY & ARCHIVE, COOPERSTOWN, N.Y.

and with that awkward — at least for me it would be awkward — hands-apart batting grip he racked up huge slugging figures. He hit those long doubles and triples in the so-called dead ball era. (I don't like that term, because it makes it sound like the ball was about as lively as a resin bag, whereas it was a "quick" dead ball from what I understand.) When Pete Rose finally overtook him in total hits in 1985, it was more a tribute to Rose's longevity than any serious challenge to Cobb's pre-eminence as the most prolific hitter of all time.

Just take a statistical snapshot of his career. It speaks for itself. He won seven of nine batting titles from 1907 to 1915 (In 1910 he lost out to Nap Lajoie by a single percentage point, .384-.383), batted .371 in 1916 and lost the title, and then won three more in a row. He accumulated 4190 hits and scored a total of 2245 runs, the most ever. But it wasn't just his hitting that made him such a devastating force. He was probably the most versatile and multidimensional of the players on my list. He won games in every imaginable way — and some you can't imagine.

Cobb was as intelligent a guy as I ever met in baseball. I always said that the two most intelligent athletes that I ever talked to — and I'd have to put Hank Greenberg in there as a very intelligent guy too — were Gene Tunney in boxing and Ty Cobb in baseball. Everything being equal, I always said those two guys would beat you because they were ahead of the game in their sports, intelligence-wise.

It is so important to have that factor of intelligence, so that you know the pitcher, know what he does, how he gets you out, what he's capable of, you know the situation of the game, you know what you did the time before, the series before. Everything works into that particular day — the wind, the elements, everything — even the catcher maybe. A guy like Cobb would have studied each catcher's style — the different way each one called his game — and could readily adjust his hitting strategy to a change of catchers. And not only was Cobb intelligent, he was also talented and completely fearless — a deadly triple threat.

On three different occasions Cobb and I got together and talked nothing but baseball. I never really did read a book on Cobb's hitting theories, but I talked to him, and there were some things that Cobb said that I personally, from my own experience, could not agree with. For example, he said when a ball was outside he stepped a little more outside, and when the ball was inside he stepped away. You can't do that! You have to plant your feet while that ball is on its way, and you can't tell whether it's inside or outside, or whether it's outside and going to break inside, or inside and going to break outside. So you have to have a happy medium all the time — and you control all that with your hands. If it's inside, you keep your hands in. If it's outside, you might have to push it out.

He held his hands three to five inches apart on the bat, and I sure couldn't hit that way, but it was probably quite conducive to his hitting .400. Sure, he probably thought he was the best ever, but why shouldn't he? He dominated everyone else during his era. He used to tell me, "Boy, Ted, if they'd pulled that shift stuff on me I'd have shown them something." He was always after me to go to left field more.

Cobb was a smart guy, and I liked him. The guy who wrote that I had a falling-out with him is full of it. We were good friends, and remained on good terms right up until the time of his death. We got along very well, and he was always very nice to me.

As I've said, he was the smartest guy I ever met in baseball, along with Hank Greenberg. But they say that on the field he was a genuine son of a bitch. (I'm just going by what they say.) Former Red Sox owner Tom Yawkey's uncle owned part of the Detroit Tigers, and he got to know Cobb and he respected Cobb so much, but when they went on a hunting trip and had a fight it broke up a friendship.

I do know that Hall of Famer Eddie Collins, who as a member of the Philadelphia A's and the Chicago White Sox played against Cobb for 22 years, revered him as a player. Eddie used to sit in the Red Sox dugout and regale us with wonderful stories about Cobb's antics. Tyrus Raymond Cobb and Babe Ruth were the two players that Collins idolized. Collins was from the old school — the Cobb era — but he had seen Babe Ruth's complete career, the whole record, and of course he realized how important Ruth had been to the game. But he also knew how important Cobb had been to the game. He had that unique perspective on the two giants of baseball.

It's no accident that Ty Cobb was the first player inducted into the Hall of Fame when it opened its doors in 1939. There's a memorable picture of three other original inductees — Ruth, Honus Wagner, and Walter Johnson — sharing the glory of the moment with various baseball notables, and it's ironic that Cobb is absent from this vanguard of American baseball heroes. It's too bad, because for many people the image that does endure is the picture of Cobb sliding into second base with his spikes sharpened and poised to maim. He represented a win-at-all-cost fanaticism that I guess our society grudgingly admires but ultimately rejects. Accurate or not, that's what people associate him with. But Cobb was the guy! You've got to put Tyrus Raymond in this book because, hell, nobody else ever did what he did.

In the late '50s, a baseball old-timer was asked by a young sports-writer how the immortal Georgia Peach, Ty Cobb, might fare in today's "new and improved" game. "Oh, he'd probably hit about .320 or so," allowed the old man. "Is that all?" shrugged the reporter. "That's not so great." "Maybe not," came the reply, "but you've got to remember he's 73 years old."

Ballpark Figures: Cobb's historic hitting feats were showcased in Detroit's Bennett Park, later to become Navin Field (now Tiger Stadium). While precise dimensions from his early career are sketchy, left field measured 345' in 1921, and centerfield fences were 467' away in 1927. Right-field barriers stood some 370' from home plate in 1921.

Lifetime Stats

Years Played: 24
Games: 3034
At-bats: 11434
Runs: 2245
Hits: 4190
Doubles: 724
Triples: 294
Home Runs: 118

Runs Batted In: 1933
Bases on Balls: 1249
Strikeouts: 357
Batting Average: .366
On Base Percentage: .432
Slugging Percentage: .512
Production: .945

Stan Musial: the kind of hitter — and the kind of man — for whom they erect statues.

AP/WIDE WORLD PHOTOS

7

Stan Musial

Career: 1941-1963

Bats: L   **Height: 6'**   **Weight: 175**

In St. Louis they erected a statue of Stan Musial frozen in that trademark stance of his: coiled and ready to hit. The inscription on the base reads, "Here stands baseball's perfect warrior. Here stands baseball's perfect knight." Well, he may not have been perfect, but he was pretty darn close. The way Stan stood at the plate, the distinctive way he wore his Cardinals cap, his easy manner when he signed autographs for kids — the way he conducted his baseball life — they all suggested a man who had escaped from a Norman Rockwell cover on the *Saturday Evening Post*. He wasn't glamorous like DiMaggio, or controversial like me. He had the image of a wholesome hero who represented the way things darn well ought to be in America. He was Andy of Mayberry with a bat, and everyone loved him.

Even though his stance might have been different, I have this feeling that Musial might have been a Joe Jackson type of hitter, because I know Jackson hit a lot of balls to left center and right center, and he hit a ton of triples. Musial was a slashing, all-around-the-ballpark hitter but he also hit to left center and certainly to right center quite a bit. That's where he could pull the ball more. And there's a guy who definitely learned how to pull the ball. When he first came up he was hitting like he had two strikes all the time, and then he got to where he was taking a pitch and waiting for a certain pitch, and finally he reached the point where he was a lot more selective. Then he got a ball he could do something with. They didn't know how to pitch him, so they'd try him inside and he'd rip the ball to right. I'm just making an educated guess when I make that comparison with Jackson. It's a theory of mine.

Just look at Musial's record. He was the best hitter in the National League for almost 20 years. The son of a gun was a .331 lifetime hitter and captured seven batting titles in the process. He also hit 475 career homers. Who says power and average don't mix? He led the National League in total bases six times and amassed 300 total bases or more 13 times. He outslugged the rest of the senior circuit on half a dozen occasions. He was as durable as he was talented, too. He played in a hundred or more games for 21 consecutive seasons — 3026 games in all. Until Aaron and Pete Rose finally surpassed him, he held most NL batting records, including most at-bats (10,972), runs scored (1949), base hits (3630), and RBIs (1951). He batted over .300 18 times, and drove in a hundred or more runs ten times. In all, he appeared in 24 All-Star games.

Musial could run — I mean he could run — which helped his hitting, but I've seen him hit all types of pitching. Every time I watched him play, he really roped them. He once hit five home runs in a doubleheader.

My son John Henry came up to me at a baseball function one time and I said, "There's Stan Musial over there, John Henry. There's one hell of a hitter!" Well, you know, he thinks that his dad is the greatest hitter who ever lived. He's convinced of that. So he said, "Do you really think he was as good a hitter as you were?" I said, "Yeah, I really think he was."

When I was at the 1960 World Series, a woman came up to me, told me I was her favorite ballplayer, and asked for my autograph. While I was signing, she casually mentioned that she was Stan Musial's mother. I told her she should be giving me her autograph.

Now Musial was a little bit different from me. I had a little more power than Stan did. If I could have run like Musial, I don't think there would have been that much comparing — but Stan Musial could run.

I played against Musial in 15 All-Star games and I played against him in one World Series, in 1946, where neither of us did very well at the plate. I've seen him play a lot of times, and even when I wasn't playing against him he was always on the newsreels. So I know that Musial was absolutely something extra. That speed of his helped him tremendously.

As a hitter Musial was a sweeper and an inside-outer and a ripper to right field. He actually had a pretty big swing, but the fact that he hit the ball to center and left center a lot actually shortened the swing enough so that he couldn't be jammed, because he was so far away from the plate anyway. The farther you hit the ball through center and left center to the opposite field to which you would pull the ball, the farther back you are when you hit the ball. So it was a little harder for Musial to pull the ball for a while. But then he got to the point where he knew that little game between the pitcher and the hitter, and he started to take full advantage of that knowledge.

He was a better all-round hitter than Hank Aaron. He won his final batting title at the age of 36, when he hit .351. And he was still among the league leaders when he was 41, hitting .330 in 1962, his next to last year. He was a hell of a hitter, and a fine all-round ballplayer. He was a quiet leader on the field and in the clubhouse and was one of the most universally respected ballplayers of our generation. He wasn't the biggest guy in the world, but he was a lithe 6', 175 lbs, and he was whippy. When he made his exit from baseball he did it with a pair of solid base hits — very little flamboyance but an abundance of style. The kind of hitter — and the kind of man — for whom they erect statues.

For a left-handed hitter, Stan Musial handled southpaw pitchers very well. Even Hall of Famer Warren Spahn, who recorded more wins (363) than any other lefty in major league history, was mere batting practice for Stan the Man. Musial batted .314 lifetime, with 14 homers against Spahn. "He's the only batter I ever intentionally walked with the bases loaded," Spahn once admitted.

Ballpark Figures: Sportsman's Park was Stan Musial's hitting ground throughout his spectacular career. The left-handed hitter faced the following dimensions: left field - 351.1'; left center - 379'; centerfield - 420'; right center - 354'; right field - 309.5'.

Lifetime Stats

Years Played: 22	**Runs Batted In:** 1951
Games: 3026	**Bases on Balls:** 1599
At-bats: 10972	**Strikeouts:** 696
Runs: 1949	**Batting Average:** .331
Hits: 3630	**On Base Percentage:** .418
Doubles: 725	**Slugging Percentage:** .559
Triples: 177	**Production:** .977
Home Runs: 475	

Shoeless Joe Jackson: there never was a better pure hitter.

NATIONAL BASEBALL LIBRARY & ARCHIVE, COOPERSTOWN, N.Y.

8

Shoeless Joe Jackson

Career: 1908-1920

Bats: L   **Height: 6'1"**   **Weight: 200**

To me it's ironic that in the Baseball Hall of Fame in Cooperstown, N.Y., the place dedicated to honoring the greatest players of the most American of all sports, there is no plaque bearing the name and likeness of Joe Jackson. No statue of Shoeless Joe. None of the bats that he once used to wreak havoc on the American League. Lord knows it's not because he wasn't good enough to be included in those hallowed halls, because his feats certainly surpass those of many of the players enshrined there. Jackson was absent only because he was accused of conspiring to fix the 1919 World Series and was banned from baseball.

Even though Jackson didn't have a long career, every record, every evidence, every comparison, everything pertaining to our selection formula gives him a high ranking. Even though he played in the dead ball era, you're still compelled to put him up there, with his high production numbers. Ty Cobb earned his place on the list with his .366 batting average and his complete domination of the league, but Jackson wasn't far behind with a .356 average and the sweetest swing imaginable. For me Jackson's hitting style was vastly superior to Cobb's. Jackson was my kind of hitter.

Using a bat he called Black Betsy, Shoeless Joe established the third-highest batting average in baseball history. Only Cobb and Hornsby (.358) were higher. In 1911, his first full major league season, Jackson hit .408 — and still he didn't win the batting title, because Cobb picked that year to hit .420! The next season Jackson batted .395 and Cobb responded with .410. Same thing in 1913, when Jackson hit .373 and Cobb .390. He was always playing in Cobb's shadow, and yet there is still no doubt in my mind as to who was the better pure hitter. With all of that statistical evidence going for him, I had to put him in this book, and I did so knowing that in the eyes of baseball he was barred as being unworthy. He was never actually convicted, but in the eyes of baseball he was guilty. I know his selection will create controversy because a lot of baseball people still feel that way. So be it. There's nothing controversial about Joe Jackson except that he was thrown out of baseball. His record is perfectly legitimate.

I didn't base my decision solely on statistical evidence. Every hitter who ever saw Joe Jackson, every player who ever saw Joe Jackson, said that he was in a class by himself. Players who played with him and against him agree on that. There was never a single one I spoke to who didn't say, "Well, he was probably the greatest hitter who ever lived." Up until his banishment in 1920, he was more revered as a hitter than even the Georgia Peach. Cobb was revered as a tough, daring, spirited, all-out, gung-ho ballplayer, and you certainly have to admire that. But Jackson — just for hitting the ball and looking good doing it — was considered the greatest. He was a classic hitter.

Personally I can't conceive of anyone looking as good with their hands three to five inches apart – like Cobb – as a guy with his hands down toward the end of the bat swinging fluidly. And that's the kind of hitter Jackson was.

I'm on the veteran selection committee for the Hall of Fame, and I brought Shoeless Joe's name up in the old-timers' meetings just to feel the committee out. Boy, there was a hell of a storm, and I could soon see they wouldn't tolerate that. God, I really got shouted down for bringing his name up for consideration. One guy especially objected. He said, "I looked it all over, Ted, and you can forget about him!"

Well, all the books are supportive of Jackson. All the records say that he tried to give the money back. He still led everybody in batting in the 1919 World Series. He hit .375 and had a good Series and all the rest of it. If he was trying to throw the Series, he did a damn poor job of it. Nevertheless, he was banned forever from the game he was born to play.

Apparently, away from the baseball diamond Jackson wasn't a very smart guy. A great hitter, but not very smart. Baseballic intelligence and street smarts are two different things. I've seen otherwise intelligent guys who could swing the bat and were pretty good hitters, and you wonder why they weren't better, and invariably it's because they were so damn dumb about what's going on at the plate. Baseballically Joe Jackson was smart. Unfortunately he wasn't very smart about a lot of other things in life.

It was a crying shame, because everybody who saw him, including Eddie Collins, who was on that Black Sox team with Jackson in 1919, said he was the best. Collins was later an executive with the Red Sox — a man who spent over 40 years of his life in baseball, a Hall of Famer who has a lifetime .333

average. Collins always compared me with Shoeless Joe, and that was such a great compliment. He said, "Ted, you're the closest thing I saw to Joe Jackson," and, "All I could think about when I saw Ted Williams was Joe Jackson." That's pretty heady stuff for a young hitter. Even today it remains one of the highest compliments I've ever received in the game of baseball: having my swing compared with Shoeless Joe's.

And Babe Ruth said he copied Joe Jackson — so you know Joe was a great hitter. Ruth was proud to have modeled his swing on Shoeless Joe's.

Obviously I never saw Shoeless Joe hit, but Collins saw that resemblance between us right away. He first saw me as a young rookie in San Diego, and I wasn't even playing at the time. I was just taking batting practice, and Collins went to the owner and asked who that kid — that left-handed hitting kid — was. "Oh, he's only a youngster who's just out of high school," Collins was told. "He's three or four years away." And still Collins said at the time, "Just give me first chance at him." And I wasn't even playing! He was really out there looking at Bobby Doerr and Georgie Myatt. That proves that Eddie Collins was as astute an observer of baseball and batters as anyone who ever lived. Not only was he a shrewd judge of opposing players, but he had that uncanny ability to assess potential in young hitters. Right away he saw something that no one else saw. He told old Bill Lane, "Just give me an option on him." And the very next year they picked me up and I went to the Red Sox. So even though I didn't see Shoeless Joe Jackson hit, Eddie Collins saw him and played alongside him, and that's good enough for me.

From anything I can ever find and read and research about Joe Jackson and his ability to hit, he stood head and shoulders above the rest. The great hitters of his day all sang his praises. He had the admiration of every player and fan until the scandal broke.

He was never around at any of the old-timers' functions, and I still regret that I never met him. For six or eight years during the '40s the Red Sox used to go through South Carolina, on our way to spring training, and the little town of Greenville, South Carolina was where Jackson lived out his remaining years. I don't know yet why Cronin didn't say to me, "Why don't you go over and see Joe Jackson and say hello to him?" Ted Williams and Joe Jackson! That would have been one hell of an interesting conversation on hitting.

But even then, more than 25 years after the scandal first broke, Jackson was a real outcast from baseball. The game turned its back on him and he was blackballed. The old-timers all knew what he had done, but he was dropped so fast and so completely from baseball that until Hollywood rediscovered him recently, most people just forgot about him. And it's too bad, because he was so damn great.

Sure he made some bad mistakes, mostly because he wasn't too smart ... but it's too bad.

Generations of fans have made the pilgrimage to Cooperstown and returned home with the mistaken impression that they have seen all the great hitters who played this game. Well, that's not quite true. That's why I'm proud to include Joe Jackson on my list of the greatest hitters of all time. On my personal field of dreams, he'd be right there in the batter's box where he belongs.

In the early days of baseball, bench jockeying was an accepted weapon for distracting opposing hitters, and some of the barbs could be exceedingly cruel. Shoeless Joe Jackson was decidedly lacking in book learning, a fact that was not lost on rival teams. As he stood at the plate awaiting the next delivery one hot August afternoon, a leather lung in the enemy dugout bellowed, "Can you spell illiterate?" Jackson responded with a stinging line drive and ended up in a cloud of dust on third base. Brushing himself off, he turned towards his tormentor and with a devilish grin asked, "Can you spell triple?"

Ballpark Figures: Shoeless Joe's original fields of dreams were League Park in Cleveland (1910-1915) and Comiskey Park in Chicago (1915-1920). League Park's dimensions were 385' to left field, 505' to deepest corner, left of center, 420' to center, and 290' to right field. Comiskey was 362' down the foul lines, 382' to the power alleys, and 420' to centerfield.

Lifetime Stats

Years Played: 13	**Runs Batted In:** 785
Games: 1330	**Bases on Balls:** 519
At-bats: 4981	**Strikeouts:** 158
Runs: 873	**Batting Average:** .356
Hits: 1772	**On Base Percentage:** .423
Doubles: 307	**Slugging Percentage** .517
Triples: 168	**Production:** .940
Home Runs: 54	

9

Hank Aaron

Career: 1954-1976

Bats: R   **Height: 6'**   **Weight: 190**

Hank Aaron didn't have that much charisma, especially compared to Mantle and Mays. The usual knock on him is that he was too quiet, too colorless, and too predictable. But remember this: a Stealth missile is quiet too, and Clark Kent was colorless until he ducked into that phone booth. As for being predictable, Rolls Royce made its reputation by producing finely tuned, predictable cars.

Aaron wasn't one of those guys who sought the limelight, and playing in places like Milwaukee and Atlanta, he didn't get that much media attention. At least not until he began to threaten Babe Ruth's 714-homer mark. That got the writers' journalistic juices flowing, and all of a sudden they wouldn't leave him alone. But he had the courage to overcome the pressures and dethrone a white American icon in the heart of the South.

Hank Aaron was one of the truly great hitters. I used to talk with the National League pitchers and they'd either talk about Aaron or Mays. The consensus seemed to be, "I don't know how to pitch to either of those two guys. They crack everything!" Some pitchers said, "I have to brush them back," or, "I have to loosen them up," or, "I've got to try to keep them honest." God, both of those guys were wonderful hitters.

For this book I am going to refer to Aaron as the "Home Run King," because he "quietly" hit more homers than anyone else. I don't think it's fair to say he's the greatest home run hitter, but he's the Home Run King and I think he'll forever have that title. He hit more home runs, 755, than any other player who will probably ever live, and he drove in 2297 runs while maintaining a .305 batting average over a 23-year major league career.

Aaron overcame the pressures and dethroned a white American icon in the heart of the South. NATIONAL BASEBALL LIBRARY & ARCHIVE, COOPERSTOWN, N.Y.

He sure had longevity, and coupled with the fact that he was a hell of a hitter, that made him the Home Run King. Like a lot of great hitters I know, with Aaron you make a mistake and he cashes in on it. I think Aaron was a classic mistake hitter.

For 20 consecutive years Aaron hit 20 or more home runs per season; for 15 seasons he topped the 30-homer mark, and eight times he hit 40 or more. He led or tied for the league lead in homers four times and drove in a hundred runs 11 times. In 1957 he captured the National League MVP award, hitting 44 home runs and driving in 132 while batting .322.

One day in spring training I was managing with Washington, and Joe Coleman was pitching for us in an exhibition against the Braves. I said, "Joe, listen. You're going to pitch against a great hitter today — Mr. Henry Aaron. Now, just have a little fun and try to see what you can do. The first time up give him nothing but breaking stuff, breaking stuff, breaking stuff." So first time up, on the third pitch he hit a ground ball to short. The next time Aaron was up, I told Joe, "Do the same thing: breaking ball, breaking ball, breaking ball." Well, he hit another ground ball to shortstop. Now the next time Aaron got up, I went to Coleman and I said, "Joe, the first pitch throw the hardest, fastest high fastball you can throw." He threw a blazing high fastball — and remember, Aaron hadn't seen one all day — and he hit a goddamn rocket out of left field. He just hammered it! That really showed me something. When he got a pitch to hit, he missed it less often than anybody else. Other guys fouled them off, or they'd take the pitch, but not Aaron. He drilled them.

They talked about the power of Aaron's wrists, and it's true he was a little "wristy," or he appeared that way. He was a great hitter, and he could get the ball in the air with a nice kind of level swing. He had great ability to get the ball in the air. You can hit howitzer shells through the infield and they're still singles, but those same shots in the air are the ultimate hits — home runs, or at least extra bases. So that puts a premium on guys like Henry Aaron who can get the ball in the air consistently.

I don't take one thing away from Aaron. I know how great a hitter he was. I also have the greatest respect for Henry Aaron as a super all-round player. But you can never make me believe that he was the best player of all time. I saw more of DiMaggio, and that's the reason I thought he was the greatest player I saw. Aaron and Musial and Mays were all super players, though, you can't deny that.

So what if Aaron played in a hitter's ballpark in Atlanta? You've got to have some advantages in your career in order to have a lot of good things happen. He sure did have longevity, but he hit consistently throughout his long career. The only thing that I can say about him as an intelligent hitter is that his record emphatically proclaims that he was. There may be some unintelligent guys who can still hit .340 for one season, but to have a successful career you've got to have that one important factor of being baseballically alert to what's going on with that pitcher and you, and what's gone on in the past.

Aaron made baseball history on the field, and now he's in the front office in Atlanta. He's one of those guys who's serious about where he wants to be in the annals of the game.

As a shy rookie from Mobile, Alabama, in 1954, Hank Aaron was an inviting target for bench jockeys and veteran players from opposing teams. Legend has it that he was once scolded by an opposing catcher for not holding the bat label toward him, as was the accepted custom of the day. Aaron's succinct reply spoke volumes about baseball's future Home Run King: "Didn't come up here to read, came up here to hit," mumbled Hammerin' Hank.

Ballpark Figures: For most of his record-breaking career, Aaron played his home games at Milwaukee's County Stadium (1954-1965) and Atlanta's Fulton County Stadium. In Milwaukee the dimensions were 320' to left field, 355' to the short alleys, 376' to the power alleys, 397' to the deep alleys, 410' to centerfield (402' starting in 1955), and 315' to right field. Fulton County Stadium was 325' down the foul lines, until 1967 when it became 330'. Left center was 385' in '66, 400' in '69, and 402' in '73. Right center was 385' in '66, 375' in '69, and 385' in '73.

Lifetime Stats

Years Played: 23	**Runs Batted In:** 2297
Games: 3298	**Bases on Balls:** 1402
At-bats: 12364	**Strikeouts:** 1383
Runs: 2174	**Batting Average:** .305
Hits: 3771	**On Base Percentage:** .377
Doubles: 624	**Slugging Percentage:** .555
Triples: 98	**Production:** .932
Home Runs: 755	

10

Willie Mays

Career: 1951-1973

Bats: R   **Height: 5'11"**   **Weight: 187**

Willie Mays was one of the most exciting and charismatic ballplayers of his era. Because of his remarkable sense of drama, and the fact that he played in larger media centers, he often overshadowed his chief National League rival, Hank Aaron. While Aaron seemed content with being the consummate ballplayer, Mays was also the consummate performer, always drawing the spotlight. They were like two sides of the same coin. You could say that Aaron had a flair for consistency while Mays had a consistent flair.

Willie Mays was an absolutely sensational, super ballplayer. He did everything well. Despite his Hall of Fame statistics, he was one of those guys you really had to see to appreciate just how good he was. He played the game with controlled abandon. On the basepaths he was in perpetual motion: stealing bases, disrupting pitchers' concentration, stretching singles into doubles, doubles into triples. He won 11 consecutive Gold Gloves, and his patented basket catches in centerfield were imitated on every sandlot in America. In the level of excitement he generated and the sheer joy he brought to his game, Mays was the Michael Jordan of the '50s and '60s. My idea would be that if DiMaggio wasn't the best all-round player I ever saw, then Mays probably was. A lot of people say that Mays was a better hitter than Aaron, but Aaron is still the home run champion. Both are just over .300 in lifetime average, with Aaron edging out Mays .305 to .302. So it's really hard to rank those two guys.

My most vivid memory of Mays is that he was a big swinger. He could swing at bad balls – and he could hit bad balls, too. He was a hard swinger. Of all the wild swingers he was probably the best, because he had extreme power. If he could get ahold of a ball – no matter where the pitch was – if he

Mays was the Michael Jordan of the '50s and '60s.

could get it in the air, it was good-bye Charlie! Yes, he swung at an awful lot of bad balls; but I even feel guilty talking like that because he was so damn great.

When he first came up in 1951 he struggled, much the same way Mantle struggled when he came up with the Yankees. Leo Durocher was able to boost his confidence, just as Stengel did for Mantle, and Mays went on to help the Giants win the pennant in his rookie year.

As I look back – and I saw Mays hit in different places – he was a lot like Mantle: if he didn't hit it well he still had a hell of a chance to get a base hit, and if he hit it well it went out of sight. He had tremendous power to all fields. I used to think he had a shot at .400. He was just one of those rare types of guys. Mantle would hit a dribbler and, hell, it was a base hit; Mays hit a dribbler and it was a base hit. Mays could run faster than Aaron, but those two guys both had the talent plus.

Mays led the National League in home runs four times, in triples three times (one tie), in hits once, and in batting once. Twice he passed the magic 50 home run barrier in a season, and he once hit four in a single game. He topped the league in on base percentage twice, in slugging percentage five times, and in overall production five times. Ten times he exceeded a hundred RBIs. He was named MVP in 1954 on the strength of a league-leading .345 average and 41 homers, leading the Giants to yet another pennant in the process. He continued his dominance well into the next decade and was named Player of the Decade for the '60s by *The Sporting News*. In 1962 he led the charge to another pennant, this time in San Francisco, and in 1965 he won another MVP award with his second 50-homer outburst.

In the All-Star game he stood out like no one else, even in the midst of those other great players. He turned it into his personal showcase and he was absolutely brilliant. He took the game seriously and helped the National League to a string of wins with his aggressive play.

Mays did some things that nobody else did. He was a muscular, stacked-up son of a gun, and yet he ran like a deer. He led the National League in stolen bases four times and finished with a total of 338 career steals. Willie was the first to hit 300 homers and steal 300 bases, pioneering that combination of power and speed that you see in today's game. I'd put Mays and Mantle in the top rank because of the devastating power both had. You're talking about almost1200 home runs between them, for God's sake.

Who would I take first on my ball club, Mantle or Mays? It would be a hell of a tough decision. You take one and I'll take the other. It's the same with

DiMaggio. You can put him with that group too. For me DiMaggio was a little smoother than either one of those guys, but he was not as awesome swinging a bat. Just smoother, more stylish.

The National League was ahead of the American League in getting the black players, and I've been all for that. My 1965 Hall of Fame induction speech at Cooperstown shows you how I felt about it. Once Jackie Robinson signed with the Brooklyn Dodgers, the entire National League benefited for years to come. Understandably, the great black players gravitated to the league that had broken the color barrier. It got some super players, including three Hall of Famers, in that era: Aaron, Frank Robinson and Willie Mays.

I still can't believe that Mays and Mantle barely hovered around the .300 mark. They are both just on the brink (Mantle just missed with .298). That's hard to believe, especially with that speed plus that both of them had. Both were free-swinging guys, two of the greatest that God ever allowed to play this game.

Willie Mays hit for power and average and roamed the outfield with the speed and grace of a gazelle. One of the most fitting compliments that he was ever paid was accorded by Bob Stevens, follow-ing a game-winning triple in the 1954 All-Star game. Wrote Stevens, "The only man who could have caught it, hit it."

Ballpark Figures: Mays played out of New York's Polo Grounds (1951-1957) and Candlestick Park in San Francisco (1958-1972). The Polo Grounds' dimensions were 279'-280' to left field, 447' to left center, 480'-483' to center, 449' to right center, and 257' to right field during his stay there. Windy Candlestick Park was 330 '-335' to left field during Mays' time there. Left center was 397' in 1960 and 365' starting in 1961. Right center was 397' in 1960 and 375' in 1961. Right field was 330' in 1960 and 335' in 1968.

Lifetime Stats

Years Played: 22
Games: 2992
At-bats: 10881
Runs: 2062
Hits: 3283
Doubles: 523
Triples: 140
Home Runs: 660

Runs Batted In: 1903
Bases on Balls: 1464
Strikeouts: 1526
Batting Average: .302
On Base Percentage: .387
Slugging Percentage: .557
Production: .944

11

Hank Greenberg

Career: 1930-1947

Bats: R　　　　**Height: 6'3½"**　　　　**Weight: 215**

Hank Greenberg destroyed the popular image of power hitters as lumbering behemoths with more brawn than brains. He was one of the most intelligent guys I ever met in baseball, and his record supports my theory that intelligence is a key ingredient in becoming a great hitter.

If Hank Greenberg could have run, he would have hit 15 points higher — and he was a .300 hitter anyway. He lost some very good years to the Second World War too, but if he'd had speed he really could have added to his record.

That's just another ingredient that helps a hitter. That's another thing about Ruth: he couldn't run that well either, but he was still a .342 hitter and he hit all those home runs. It's scary to think he could have been even more devastating with speed. Same thing with Greenberg. You can't deny that it would have added to their legend.

During an abbreviated career than spanned parts of 13 seasons with Detroit and Pittsburgh, Greenberg stroked 331 home runs while maintaining a .313 batting average. The towering 6'3½", 215-lb first baseman captured five American League home run titles, batted .300 nine times, and led the league in RBIs on four separate occasions, including a 183-RBI outburst in 1937. He hit a dramatic grand slam against the St. Louis Browns to clinch the 1945 pennant for the Tigers on the last day of the season. In all, he led the Tigers to four American League pennants and hit well over .300 in World Series play. When he was later traded to Pittsburgh, he was instrumental in helping Ralph Kiner hone his Hall of Fame hitting skills.

Of all the big hitters that I talked to, I probably talked more with Greenberg alone than with any other hitter, but the funny part of it was, his

Hank Greenberg was one of the most intelligent guys I ever met in baseball.

NATIONAL BASEBALL LIBRARY & ARCHIVE, COOPERSTOWN, N.Y.

questions weren't about how you swung or how you hit a high ball or a low ball or anything like that. He was a great hitter himself and he didn't need to know that. No, he wanted to talk about every pitcher in the league, and he was always asking, "How'd that pitcher pitch to you?" I'm sure he wasn't worried about telling the Tigers what I was telling him, but he wanted to hear what I had to say.

He was always rated as a smart hitter. Pitchers knew that you didn't give him too much of the same thing, because he'd lay for it and he'd hit it. Probably the only ball that he couldn't defend against all the time was that extra-good high fastball. They thought they could pitch him high and tight. I know that. The pitchers all wanted to throw him their best fastball. And you know, I think even DiMaggio would say, "Show me a guy who can really buzz that high fastball and he's going to be kind of tough." But a high fastball to Greenberg — as good as he was — and a high fastball to DiMaggio were two different things. With Joe you'd better get it within an eight- or ten-inch circle or he'd nail you. His area of vulnerability was smaller than Greenberg's.

But as I've said, Greenberg was very smart. He'd usually take that pitch for a ball, or the pitcher would make a mistake and he'd get a base hit. And he'd hang in there, and next time up they'd make another mistake and he'd hit the long ball. I thought Feller was the greatest pitcher of my time, and I really think Greenberg thought so too. He'd say, "Jeez, that son of a gun is something else, isn't he?" That was the nature of my conversations with him. He spoke in general terms and didn't divulge too much. I thought Greenberg was a great guy.

My most vivid memory of Greenberg was that he'd hit a ball to the outfield and you'd think that you had it, and it would go back, back, back into the upper deck. A lot of times Greenberg would hit a fly ball to me in Detroit and my first reaction was, "Oh, I'll get that," and damn it, it goes deep into the seats. He didn't look like he'd smacked it that hard. It just had that little undercarry like Foxx, Hank Sauer, Wally Post, and Wally Berger could give — Pat Seerey and Killebrew had it too. But Greenberg had the loftiest ball in the majors. Yes, he was a great hitter!

Hank's got 331 lifetime homers, but there's no question he would have hit 500 home runs, because he missed some of his best years and only managed 5193 at-bats. He was one of the first players in the American League to be drafted in 1941, so he missed four and a half years! And then he came back and led the Tigers' charge to the 1945 American League flag. I was a young player when he went to war. Those were big years for him to miss, because when he came back he didn't quite have it and he was on his way down then. His last two or three years were not quite up to his standards, despite the homers.

Greenberg's intelligence was a key to his success. That comes under the last category that a successful hitter needs: courage, eyesight, power, timing, and intelligence. It's more than being a guess hitter. It's proper thinking. I sure think that today's hitters are lacking in that last category: intelligence. They're lacking mostly in that last one. I can sit there in a game as a spectator and start talking to you about the players and the count, and yet the batter, who should be most aware of the situation, gets the count right to hit and he fouls the pitch off or he's late. He misses! What's to blame?

I know that I'm not smart, but the thing that made it possible for me to improve was that I did so much hitting that through trial and error I learned. I realized that when I fouled it off I'd have to be quicker. I realized what I'd done wrong on a swing — whether I'd gotten too big with a swing, for example, that type of thing. That's why Greenberg was a hell of a player: smart, calculating, a guess hitter who was always a step ahead of the pitcher.

Hank Greenberg could do it all. He hit the ball a ton, crushed it like few have ever done. Unfortunately his career was one of the casualties of the war. Nevertheless, the impact he made in just 1394 games is nothing short of amazing.

In 1938 Hank Greenberg came within two home runs of matching Babe Ruth's record 60-homer performance of 1927. With two games left in the season, Greenberg's quest fizzled in Cleveland's cavernous League Park, where the left-field fence was 375 feet from home plate. As if this weren't enough of a challenge for the big right-hander, on the final day of the season Greenberg had the misfortune of facing his nemesis Bob Feller, who proceeded to fan a record 18 Tigers.

Ballpark Figures: Greenberg, a right-handed power hitter, played virtually his entire career in Navin Field/Briggs Stadium in Detroit. Left field fluctuated between 367' and 340' during Greenberg's playing days. Left center was 365' in 1942, and centerfield varied between 464' and 440'. Right center was 370' in 1942, and right field shrank from 367' to 325'.

Lifetime Stats

Years Played: 13
Games: 1394
At-bats: 5193
Runs: 1051
Hits: 1628
Doubles: 379
Triples: 71
Home Runs: 331

Runs Batted In: 1276
Bases on Balls: 852
Strikeouts: 844
Batting Average: .313
On Base Percentage: .412
Slugging Percentage: .605
Production: 1.017

12

Mickey Mantle

Career: 1951-1968

Bats: L & R **Height: 6'** **Weight: 201**

Mickey Mantle was the very prototype of popularity. He had those blond good looks, that infectious grin, and a kind of farm-bred humility that melted the hearts of even the most cynical New Yorkers. It was ironic because he came out of Commerce, Oklahoma, as a shy kid, and yet he put his mark on one of the world's most sophisticated cities. The big city didn't change him that much. His popularity went well beyond the Big Apple, though. He transformed even the most ardent Yankee-haters across the length and breadth of the country. For 18 glorious summers it was almost like Mickey was the poster boy for baseball — if not for America. Every time you looked up you saw his face on one magazine cover or another. Even today his name is gold.

When he broke into the majors, I wasn't all that impressed with Mr. Mantle. That came a little later. In his rookie year, everyone was talking about this young phenom like he was the second coming of the Babe. Well, I saw Mantle break in and I saw what Mickey did — or failed to do — in lots and lots of games. Now I always thought that I could appraise hitters, and I thought that I knew a lot about what a guy was going to do even after seeing him only a few times. Others envied the way Mantle could swing, but I talked about the way he missed. And he did miss, and I came close to saying — and I did say it in my own mind — "I'm not sure this guy is going to make enough contact to make it in the majors." But then Mantle started to make a little more contact, and then he started to really bust them, and all of a sudden he was on his way.

Now Casey Stengel was his manager at that time, and Casey was smart. He took Mickey out of the lineup before he broke all records for strikeouts. A

Mickey Mantle was the very prototype of popularity. BETTMANN ARCHIVE

rookie needs to be protected like that. When he returned to the lineup he started to make solid contact and started to hit them where few people have ever hit them. And all of a sudden he was making baseball history.

Mantle was power personified. If you had to fault a great hitter like Mantle it was that he wouldn't concede a thing with two strikes. You've got to concede with two strikes. It's hard for me to conceive of Mickey Mantle falling short of a .300 lifetime average. And Mr. Mays barely making it! Two of the greatest God ever let play this game and they're barely in the .300 range. They both possessed tremendous speed, tremendous power, but they were both free-swinging guys who missed the ball an awful lot. It's really not taking too much away from them, but they absolutely should have been better hitters for average.

Mickey hardly knew what protecting the plate was. He didn't know what conceding to the pitcher meant. He didn't know that you had to hit certain pitchers a little differently than you did certain other pitchers. And despite all that, he was one of the greatest sluggers in baseball history.

That's the biggest difference between Mantle and Mays and Joe DiMaggio. Mantle and Mays didn't concede much with two strikes, but you take a great hitter like DiMaggio; he conceded — even though he might come up a little bit on the bat — but he would try not to pull the ball quite so much. Mays and Mantle didn't seem too concerned with that kind of strategy. They continued to swing for the fences regardless of the count.

Mantle once told a sportswriter about a discussion he'd had with me. We had been talking about hitting, and Mickey said, "Honestly, when I got through talking with Ted I didn't know what the hell he was talking about." I had to laugh. He was a little different type of hitter. He was always swinging from the heels. He was strong and he was quick. Jimmie Foxx was pretty near the same type of hitter as Mickey, but Mickey wasn't nearly as smart a hitter as Jimmie was. Jimmie was pretty damn smart. He had a baseball mind. He knew every pitcher and how they'd pitch to him, and even though he'd strike out as much as anybody, he had a good idea what the pitcher was trying to do to him. He hit them a ton just like Mick, but he was a more consistent, more disciplined hitter.

Now I'm not saying that Mickey didn't improve and adjust. It's a matter of degree. When you're up 8000 times you mature and you learn some things at the plate, mostly through the process of trial and error. He was a great change-of-speed hitter, and after a while he knew he wasn't going to get those pitches too much anymore. So he adjusted. And after a while he knew where they were going to pitch to him. Then he got his strike zone down and consolidated a little bit, and all of a sudden he was the most feared hitter in baseball.

Mantle possessed that rare combination of power and speed. They called him the Commerce Comet. He was once timed at 3.1 seconds to first base, and that resulted in countless leg hits. He hit .365 in 1957, and that year he had something like 49 infield hits. Mickey bunted with two strikes a lot that year so he wouldn't strike out, and we on the Red Sox were thankful to God that he'd do that. He'd get a hit every time but at least the ball stayed in the ballpark; he probably could have hit .500 that way, because he was on his way to first with everyone playing back and so he had a hell of a chance.

Mantle once said that if they'd been talking about 40/40 (40 home runs and 40 stolen bases in the same year) when he played, then hell, he'd have done 40/40. But at that time they didn't talk about that statistic. Now they have statistics on everything. They keep statistics on the last eight games you played, for Pete's sake. "He's only hitting .262," they say, "but he's hitting .466 in his last eight games." It's gotten ridiculous.

Mantle had tremendous power and he drove in a truckload of runs. That's why the most natural comparison was with Foxx. Mantle and Foxx were both built the same and I've got to feel that they both generated great bat speed. Mickey was the only other hitter I saw who made the bat-on-ball sound that Jimmie Foxx made when he hit it. It was so distinctive that a blind man could pick out a Foxx or Mantle home run.

Mantle was the greatest switch-hitter this game will ever see. I'm talking about combining power with average. It was a skill his father taught him and he worked damn hard to master it. He hit them as far as anybody either way. In my opinion he was a better pure hitter right-handed even though he usually batted left. He was a legitimate home run threat from both sides of the plate, hitting 373 of his 536 lifetime homers left-handed and 163 from the right side. In 1956, when he won his only Triple Crown, he had 357 at-bats from the left side and 176 from the right. He had 39 homers, 99 RBIs, and a .342 average left-handed and 13 homers, 31 RBIs, and a .375 average right-handed. That's a pretty good balance.

On ten different occasions Mantle hit home runs from both sides of the plate during the same game. He pretty well inspired the term "tape-measure home run" through his prodigious clouts. He once came within a whisker of hitting a ball clean out of Yankee Stadium, launching a 600-foot rocket off Pedro Ramos of the Washington Senators. But regardless of the distance, he never showed the pitcher up by standing at home plate to admire his "dinger" like they do today; he ran out each homer with his head down.

What talent he had! And he was a hell of a humble guy, with all that he did. When he captured the Triple Crown in '56, he had a great .353 average, 130 RBIs and 52 home runs, the first of two times he would go over the 50-homer mark. He won three MVP awards and led the American League in homers four times, in slugging four times, and in walks five times. Ten times he batted over .300.

One of the great records anyone will ever have and one that will never be beaten is his 18 home runs in the World Series. In the first place, no one is going to get into the World Series as often as those guys on the Yankees did. Never. He played in 12 of them, and also holds the Series records for most RBIs (40) and runs scored (42).

In 1961 Roger Maris was batting third, ahead of Mantle, and that gave Roger a big advantage in his quest to break the 60-homer mark. With Mickey waiting in the on-deck circle, there's little wonder that Roger wasn't accorded a single intentional walk that entire season. After all, Mantle hit .317, stroked 54 homers, and drove in 128 runs that year. The pitchers were forced to pitch to Maris and he saw some good offerings. Now you might argue that with Maris' 61 homers that year, Mantle was up a lot of times with no one on base. Well, Maris had almost a hundred other hits in 1961, and 94 walks, so he was still on base a lot for Mick to drive him in. There's still no question that it's a big advantage to hit behind a big hitter. The fourth batter has the biggest advantage in the lineup, I think, for runs batted in.

With all his natural gifts, the tragic flaw in Mantle's dramatic career was his proneness to injury. He underwent surgery on both knees, along with shoulder operations and numerous and well-documented leg ailments. His ankles were notoriously weak and apparently hampered his effectiveness from the left side. The fact that he often played in severe pain has only added to his legend.

Aside from these physical complaints, Mickey also had what I feel was a chronic Achilles' heel: his unwillingness to concede with two strikes and his tendency to strike out. Even so, his batting average stands at .298, just below the magic .300 mark. No list of great hitters would be complete without the name Mickey Mantle.

In my opinion Aaron was a better hitter than Mays or Mantle, and he had pretty good speed too, but not the speed of a Mays or a Mantle. For hitting the ball, I'd have to take Aaron over the other two. For power and speed I think that Mantle and Mays are right there together. Tremendous ability, all three of those guys.

Mickey Mantle was one of the game's premier sluggers but was prone to strikeouts. With typical self-deprecating humor, the Commerce Comet put his whiffs in new perspective. "You've gotta think that the average fella is gonna come up to the plate maybe 550 times during the course of a normal season," he said. "Looking at my 1710 Ks, I figure that during three of my 18 years I did absolutely nothin'."

Ballpark Figures: The switch-hitting Mick played all of his home games at Yankee Stadium. Left field was 301' down the line, gradually expanding to 402', 415', and finally 457' in deepest left center. The fences were a prodigious 466' at the left of the centerfield screen, 461' in center, and 407' in right center. Right field was 295'-296'.

Lifetime Stats

Years Played: 18	**Runs Batted In:** 1509
Games: 2401	**Bases on Balls:** 1734
At-bats: 8102	**Strikeouts:** 1710
Runs: 1677	**Batting Average:** .298
Hits: 2415	**On Base Percentage:** .423
Doubles: 344	**Slugging Percentage:** .557
Triples: 72	**Production:** .979
Home Runs: 536	

13

Tris Speaker

Career: 1907-1928

Bats: L   **Height: 5'11½"**   **Weight: 193**

Speaker was one of the true greats of all time. They never spoke about a centerfielder in the same breath as Tris Speaker until Joe DiMaggio, and then Willie Mays, came along. Because nobody could do what Speaker could do. He had the great range in the outfield and he could hit like hell. He was the epitome of endurance, playing a hundred or more games for 19 consecutive years.

He was American League MVP in 1912 for Boston, but his best offensive performance came when he was peddled to Cleveland for $50,000 in 1916 and promptly led the AL with a .386 average and 211 hits, tying for the league lead with 41 doubles. In fact he topped the AL in two-base hits eight times and finished with a grand total of 793, an American League record. From 1909 onward he batted over .300 18 years out of 20, and he hit .350 or better nine times. The big Texan is generally acknowledged as one of the two or three best defensive centerfielders in baseball history.

Speaker was the first to play a really shallow centerfield. He always claimed that Cy Young taught him to be a great fielder. Apparently Young used to hit fungos to Speaker hour after hour after hour — until he could anticipate where the ball was going to go before he even hit it.

I'm not sure who taught him to hit, but Speaker definitely belongs on the top-25 Hit List. I'm sorry to say I never talked the specifics of hitting with him. At the time I was hitting like a son of a bitch, and they were trying everything to get me out, including pulling that switch on me. And Speaker gave me the greatest compliment of all the great players that I knew — not once or twice but several times. He said, "You're the greatest hitter of them all." And he played with Gehrig and Ruth and Cobb and Jackson. Other

Speaker was among the aristocracy of hitters.

NATIONAL BASEBALL LIBRARY & ARCHIVE, COOPERSTOWN, N.Y.

people have paid me compliments, but I admired that man so much that it meant a lot to me.

Collins revered Speaker, and Collins was my closest touch to the oldest players. He played with them and against them. He played in the dead ball era and in the lively ball era too. He didn't quit until the late '20s, so he's got that broad experience. He saw all the great hitters. He told me that Speaker hardly ever struck out, and when I looked it up he sure was right about that. He struck out a total of 220 times in his 22-year career. Hell, that's ten times a season. Some players do that in a week.

Speaker's career paralleled Cobb's, and as a result his hitting credits have been somewhat overshadowed, if not ignored. However, being second to Ty Cobb still places you in very select company and is sure no reason to hang your head. He hit .344 lifetime to Cobb's .366, but he hit .370 or better six times and accumulated 3514 base hits with Boston and Cleveland. Only once did he top Cobb for the American League batting crown, hitting .386 in 1916 to Cobb's .371.

Speaker wasn't a little guy; he was a nicely built guy of about 6' and 193 lbs. He was put together pretty damn well. I do think that Tris Speaker was capable of doing a little bit more as a hitter than he did, because he played almost ten years in the lively ball era and still didn't hit as many home runs as he should have. Apparently he was a line drive type hitter, and his record number of doubles would indicate that. He also hit 223 triples, which is good for eighth on the all-time list. He held his bat low and protected the plate. Home runs were not a big priority for him, I guess, but he used his great speed to steal 433 bases in his career.

Personally I think it was just the idea that average — except in the case of Ruth and Foxx and Gehrig and a few others — was the main thing they strove for. Still, you can't deny the fact that there must have been more good hitters in those days. These guys kept the high averages over an entire career. George Brett did it one year, another guy did it one year, but the guys on my Hit List kept doing it over an entire career.

The other interesting thing about Tris Speaker is that he was a natural right-hander but had to bat and throw left because of a broken arm he got after being thrown from a horse as a teenager back in Texas. Despite the injury, he started out his career as a pitcher before finally settling in centerfield.

Speaker was dubbed the Gray Eagle because of his distinctive hair color and distinguished manner. He was considered to be part of the aristocracy of baseball, and in my mind he also belongs in the aristocracy of hitters.

Despite being on opposite sides in a divisive feud between rival factions on the 1915 Red Sox, Babe Ruth later picked Tris Speaker as the centerfielder on his all-time team. Ruth called Speaker "a fifth infielder" and insisted that he had actually seen him throw runners out at first on more than one occasion. As a pitcher, Ruth had good reason to admire Speaker, and not only for his defensive skills. Ironically, the man who was later to become the most devastating hitter in the history of the game depended on the Gray Eagle for most of the Red Sox offense as well.

Ballpark Figures: The Gray Eagle's home nests were at Fenway Park in Boston and League Park in Cleveland. League Park was 376' to left field. Left of centerfield measured 450', centerfield was 420', right center was 400', and right field was 290'.

Lifetime Stats

Years Played: 22	**Runs Batted In:** 1559
Games: 2789	**Bases on Balls:** 1381
At-bats: 10208	**Strikeouts:** 220
Runs: 1881	**Batting Average:** .344
Hits: 3515	**On Base Percentage:** .424
Doubles: 793	**Slugging Percentage:** .500
Triples: 223	**Production:** .924
Home Runs: 117	

14

Al Simmons

Career: 1924-1944

Bats: R   **Height: 6'**   **Weight: 210**

Al Simmons had as much raw power at the plate as anyone who ever played the game. I saw enough of him when he was in uniform during his last days as a major league player and coach in Philadelphia to know that. When I looked at Simmons he reminded me of Gargantua. Of all the hitters that I saw with a bat, he looked the most menacing. Not big and heavy, just BIG! Big arms, big hands — a big, strong, burly guy. He had a bat as long as a barge pole and he'd stride up to the plate with that thing and scare you to death. I never saw him play when he was at his peak, but he sure impressed me just to look at him.

Simmons never got the publicity of a Foxx or a Gehrig or a Ruth, but of everybody I ever talked to, I don't know a man who didn't say, "Whew, Simmons is a better hitter than Foxx, except that Foxx had that flair to hit." Over the years I've also heard people say that Joe Jackson was better than Cobb, or Gehrig was better than Ruth — and many who have insisted that Simmons outranked Foxx. But the records don't indicate that. He didn't have the power of Foxx or DiMaggio. And yet Simmons was a .334 hitter and, if your team needed a base hit, he was just about as good as any right-hander who ever went up to the plate.

He didn't make the magazine covers like Foxx and other stars of his time. My own impression is that he was a big guy who wasn't too personable, whereas Foxx was extremely popular. He didn't have much of a personality — and he didn't have too much regard for anybody. Simmons and Cobb were both critical of me for taking a pitch an inch or an inch and a half off the plate. Today when a hitter does it, he's got "great patience; no wonder he's a great hitter." Boom, boom, boom. But Simmons and Cobb were always lambasting me. Why Cobb would do that I don't know, but he was another guy who wasn't too personable. Now when they ask me to compare present-day hitters like Boggs and Mattingly, I say Boggs is a better hitter day in and day out, mainly because he's more selective at the plate. He's a pretty smart hitter. He makes the pitcher pitch. If he's fooled he doesn't fool with it. When he's got two strikes, he'll go inside-out, inside-out. He's right there all the time. I certainly don't criticize him, like Simmons did me, for being selective at the plate.

The only time I ever really talked to Al Simmons was when he said, "How much you wanna bet you don't hit .400?" This was on the eve of the last day of the season in 1941. Now when I'd go into Detroit that year, Harry Heilmann would come on out to see me and he was as friendly as hell. He'd visit with his old friend Joe Cronin and then he'd sit down with me and give me that little resumé of his. He'd say, "Don't you worry about that right-field fence. You just hit the way you can hit!" But when I talked to Simmons, he swaggered down through the Boston dugout and said, "How much you wanna bet you don't hit .400?" I don't think Simmons meant anything by it; he was just that type of individual. Meanwhile, Heilmann was just encouraging the hell out of me.

Simmons was known as "Bucketfoot," and they claim his left foot was pointed down the line as if he wanted to take a shortcut to third base, but his stance wasn't that unorthodox, despite what's been written. He was big and rugged and he stepped out at the plate a little bit, but his rear end and hands were always right there. You can step out and, hell, still be right there, ready to hit.

He warmed up with a .308 average in his rookie year and went on to total 253 hits and a .387 average in his sophomore season; and all of a sudden his batting stance didn't look so strange. In fact I put him right up there with Musial and Mays. He certainly belongs in the first rank.

Simmons topped the American League in 1930 with a .381 mark and repeated the feat in 1931 with a .390 average. He was the AL's MVP in 1929 with a .365 average, 34 home runs and a league-leading 157 RBIs. He led the league in hits twice and fell just short of the exclusive 3000 hit club, finishing with 2927 in 20 seasons.

He was strong, but he was also a skilled batsman. I don't know why he didn't hit for a bigger career average. Four times his average was over .380. You take four of the best years from any player that ever lived and compare them with Simmons' best. That's a good project: find out if any player, other than Cobb with his .420, .410, .401, and .390, and Harry Heilmann, averaged over .380 for four years or better — and twice hit .390. How many

When I looked at Simmons he reminded me of Gargantua. BETTMANN ARCHIVE

players have ever done that? You get that one together and you'll find out that there weren't many players like that. It's a pretty elite club. They could hold their meetings in a phone booth, there were so few.

Al Simmons was as good as there ever was, but he played in Philadelphia and no one paid any attention to what he did there. He had none of Foxx's flair, and he sure didn't hit them as far. No one will ever convince me that Simmons was as good as Foxx, but, just like Frank Robinson, he was a terribly underrated player.

Aloysius Szymanki, better known to baseball fans as Al Simmons, was hardly a textbook hitter. Critics gave him the nickname "Bucketfoot" because of his awkward tendency to pull away from pitchers towards the dugout. New York Times sportswriter Arthur Daley referred to him as "Unquestionably . . . the worst-looking of all top hitters. His style was atrocious. . . . He should have been a sucker for an outside pitch. He wasn't. . . . Curves should have troubled him. They didn't. In fact, he was the deadliest clutch hitter on the great Athletics team."

Ballpark Figures: The right-handed Simmons played most of his career (nine full seasons) at Shibe Park in Philadelphia. Left field was 334' (1922-1925), and changed to 312' in 1926 and to 334' in 1930. Left center was 387' from 1922 to '24, changing to 405' in 1925. Centerfield was 468' during Simmons' career. Right center was 393'; right field was 380' from 1921 to '25, changing to 307' in 1926 and to 331' in 1930. Simmons also played in Chicago, Detroit, Washington, and Boston of the AL, with short stints in Boston and Cincinnati of the NL.

Lifetime Stats

Years Played: 20	**Runs Batted In:** 1827
Games: 2215	**Bases on Balls:** 615
At-bats: 8759	**Strikeouts:** 737
Runs: 1507	**Batting Average:** .334
Hits: 2927	**On Base Percentage:** .380
Doubles: 539	**Slugging Percentage:** .535
Triples: 149	**Production:** .915
Home Runs: 307	

15

Johnny Mize

Career: 1936-1953

Bats: L   Height: 6'2"   Weight: 215

Mize was one of the really outstanding hitters in baseball history. Every place he went, he hit. He was one of only a handful of players to hit 50 homers in a season, and he did it in New York at the Polo Grounds, a park that for a hitter like Mize was even harder than Sportsman's Park in St. Louis, where he spent most of his career. Then he moved over to Yankee Stadium and hit there too. Every place he played, from the time he started to play baseball till the time he quit, he was a premier hitter.

When he ambled up to the plate people expected big things because he made things happen. I always thought he was one of the very best. In the book I wrote 25 years ago, *The Science of Hitting*, I said Johnny Mize was one of the greatest hitters of all time and he deserved to be in the Hall of Fame. It took them 12 years after that for them to put him in.

Mize was a big, burly guy who nevertheless had a smooth, effortless swing. He was another of those hitters who studied his craft and had a thorough knowledge of pitchers and their repertoire. He had to find some edge, because he was a .312 hitter and he didn't help himself very much running. He hit as high as .364 one year, although he couldn't run a lick. Imagine that: he got no leg hits, and he still hit .300. What would he have done with speed?

Mize burst upon the major league scene with a .329 average, 19 homers, and 93 RBIs in his rookie campaign, good enough to capture unofficial rookie of the year honors for 1936 (the official Rookie of the Year Award began in 1940). He was the National League batting champion in my rookie year of 1939, with a .349 average. In total he led or tied for the league lead in homers four times, and was the RBI king three times. He went on to hit a total of 359 home runs in his 15-year major league career, but lost three prime

Mize hit .364 one year and couldn't run a lick. CHICAGO TODAY

years to the war. Although he never won the MVP award, he was in the running several times and finished second in the voting twice.

Mize hit three home runs in a game on a record six different occasions, and four times he hit three consecutive homers in one game. His greatest power binge came when he muscled a career-high 51 in 1947, to set a single-season NL record for left-handed hitters. That same year he had a slugging average of .614 and drove in 138 runs. In all, Mize captured four slugging titles, and during his career he also boasted league highs in doubles, triples, and runs scored.

His lifetime slugging percentage is .562, second to Rogers Hornsby in National League history and eighth best overall. Eight times he drove in a hundred or more runs, and he batted over .300 from his rookie campaign in 1936 until 1948. He topped the 20-homer mark eight out of nine years and nine times in his career. Like many ballplayers of his era, he lost three key years to World War II.

I knew from talking to him that he knew that little game that went on between pitcher and hitter. That's what helped make him a superior hitter. He talked a great deal more about hitting than DiMaggio did, for example. He really made an impact as a pinch hitter with the Yankees. I know he impressed our Red Sox club. You just held your breath when he lumbered up to bat. In a close game you really had to be worried about him, because if he didn't hit a home run, the son of a gun would draw a walk and put a guy on.

Mize was enormously strong. They called him the "Big Cat" because of smooth fielding around first base, but he also had that fluid swing that generated great bat speed and tremendous power. He could handle the best kind of fastball and the meanest curves equally well — a fine hitter who was very underrated, probably because he lost those key years to the armed services and didn't hit 500 home runs. He was a quiet guy who wasn't that popular with the press, but he was finally named to the Hall of Fame in 1980. In my opinion it was long overdue.

In the classic 1952 cross-town World Series between the New York Yankees and the Brooklyn Dodgers, Johnny Mize turned in a memorable hitting performance. He pinch-hit a homer in game three and contributed another in a game-four Yankee victory the next afternoon. He followed with a third round-tripper in as many days in an extra-inning loss in game five. Mize batted a lofty .400 in the Series.

Ballpark Figures: During his peak years the left-handed Mize divided his time between two home parks: Sportsman's Park in St. Louis (1936-1941) and the Polo Grounds in New York (1942-1949). Sportsman's Park offered a 310' target in right field, 354' in right center, and 420' in center. Left center was 379' and left field was a 351' poke. The Polo Grounds' right-field fence was 257' away, right center was 440'-449', and centerfield fluctuated between 505' and 448' during his stay. Left center was 455' and left field was 280'.

Lifetime Stats

Years Played: 15	**Runs Batted In:** 1337
Games: 1884	**Bases on Balls:** 856
At-bats: 6443	**Strikeouts:** 524
Runs: 1118	**Batting Average:** .312
Hits: 2011	**On Base Percentage:** .397
Doubles: 367	**Slugging Percentage:** .562
Triples: 83	**Production:** .959
Home Runs: 359	

16

Mel Ott

Career: 1926-1947

Bats: L   **Height: 5'9"**   **Weight: 170**

Mel Ott was the first hitter who I ever heard say, "I don't look for fastballs as much as some hitters. I look for breaking stuff." When I read that I wondered why, and he explained, "They just don't throw me many fastballs, so why would I be looking for that all the time?" That's the same theory I applied when I was looking for the slider for 15 years.

Ott's stance was a little peculiar, a little different from everyone else's, but it's results that count. He was a real slugger, and I think that of all the hitters in baseball, Ott probably best adapted himself and his style to conform to his abilities. He could pull the ball, but his greatest skill was being able to conform to the greatest advantage to the park he hit in. And that's where his detractors come in.

The biggest knock on Ott has always been that he hit 323 of his 511 home runs in that generous little bandbox known as the Polo Grounds. He used to bail out by pulling away from the first-base line, but it worked to his advantage because he was a pull hitter hitting in the Polo Grounds with that short right field porch just 257 feet away. And he crowded the plate so much that even if he did have his foot in the bucket, he still protected the plate with his bat.

Hell, he was a little guy — at 5'9", 170 lbs, the smallest guy on my Hit List — but still he was the second guy to ever hit 500 home runs, and one of only six to do it while maintaining a .300 batting average. He hit like he was ten feet tall. No wonder they called him "the Little Giant." That tells me something about his ability to adapt. He got the maximum return from his physical and mental abilities. You've got to give him a hell of a lot of credit for that, regardless of where he played.

Mel Ott: no wonder they called him "the Little Giant." NATIONAL BASEBALL LIBRARY & ARCHIVE, COOPERSTOWN, N.Y.

He led or tied for the league lead in home runs on six occasions, and nine times in his 22-year career he exceeded one hundred RBIs.

A writer once asked him the obvious question: "Where did you get all that power?" His answer impressed me. "Timing, I guess you'd call it. Mostly it was a matter of connecting at exactly the right place in the swinging arc. That way I was able to get every pound behind the bat." (From *Sport Magazine*'s "All-Time All Stars," by Al Stump.) Timing. That's one of my five ingredients that make a great hitter.

Eddie Collins said that Ott used to choke up on the bat a lot for a power hitter. They said he had a little snap swing like Cobb or Wee Willie Keeler. He must have had awfully powerful wrists.

My old manager Joe Cronin had a lot of respect for Ott. Ott beat Cronin's Washington Senators with a dramatic homer off a left-handed pitcher in the opener of the 1933 World Series. And then he won the Series for the Giants with an extra-inning clout in the fifth game. He hit .389 in that Series.

Ott twice scored six runs in a single game, which is a hell of a feat, but in the game that really shows what rival pitchers thought of Mel Ott, he didn't lift his bat from the shoulder once. On October 5, 1929, he was accorded five intentional walks, a league record. Now that's the kind of respect only a Babe Ruth-caliber player commands. He also set the National League record for most bases on balls with 1708 (since broken by Joe Morgan) and most years with a hundred or more bases on balls (10). He was obviously patient at the plate and had a sharp hitter's eye.

Ott owned a variety of National League hitting marks until they were eventually surpassed by Mays and Aaron and others. Forty-nine times he hit two or more homers in a game. For five consecutive seasons, he powered 30 or more homers.

Referring to Ott, Leo Durocher once said, "Nice guys finish last." Leo was wrong. He finishes 16th on my list of all-time great hitters.

Chuck Klein and Mel Ott battled to the wire for the 1929 National League home run crown. Klein held a narrow 43-42 margin when his Phillies and Ott's Giants met in a season-ending doubleheader. In a flagrant display of misguided loyalty, the Phillie pitchers insured their teammate's victory by walking Ott five times, including once with the bases loaded.

Ballpark Figures: The New York Giants star played his home games at the Polo Grounds. Left field varied between 279' and 280' during his career. Left center was 447' to the left of the bullpen and 455' to the right. Centerfield fluctuated wildly between 430' and 505'. Right center was 440' to 449', and right field was approximately 257'.

Lifetime Stats

Years Played: 22	**Runs Batted In:** 1860
Games: 2730	**Bases on Balls:** 1708
At-bats: 9456	**Strikeouts:** 896
Runs: 1859	**Batting Average:** .304
Hits: 2876	**On Base Percentage:** .414
Doubles: 488	**Slugging Percentage:** .533
Triples: 72	**Production:** .947
Home Runs: 511	

17

Harry Heilmann

Career: 1914-1932

Bats: R   **Height: 6'1"**   **Weight: 200**

Harry Heilmann's first few years were just ordinary — and then he came on like dynamite. Cobb was the one who made him a better hitter, when he took over as manager of the Tigers in 1921. Heilmann told me personally,

> *When Cobb taught me how to hit inside-out, from then on I was never afraid to get two strikes on me. I could wait that much longer and still inside-out it and get the big part of the bat on the ball enough to drive it over the infielders. I didn't fear having two strikes on me after I learned that. I didn't try to pull the ball. I was aiming it through the middle, and if I had to go inside-out a little bit to get it through the middle, to get the big part of the bat on the ball — BANG — I could do it.*

So he became a great hitter when Cobb taught him to go inside-out with his swing. His average just soared. That's a very important swing, and I mention it in *The Science of Hitting*. A hitter has got to learn that swing to survive, and the best way to learn it is by hitting "pepper." When you get an inside ball, keep your hands out in front of the bat and push it back through the middle. Your arms aren't completely extended like in the power swing and you don't break your wrists. You're protecting the plate. It was the answer for me and it was Cobb's gift to Harry Heilmann. It's an easier way to hit, and it gives you the time to get the meat of the bat on the ball.

Heilmann's lifetime average was .342. He must have been an incredible hitter because how else could he have brought his average up to that level after four sub-par years at the start of his career? He hit under .300 his first

Harry Heilmann: the last American Leaguer before me to hit .400.

four seasons in the majors. He rallied to hit .320 in 1919 and .309 in 1920 and then went on a ten-year hitting spree after Cobb took him under his wing in 1921. He was Cobb's star pupil, leading the league with a .394 average in his freshman year under Tyrus and "graduating" with a .400 average (.403) in 1923. That's like a Ph.D. for a hitter.

Heilmann was the last American Leaguer before me to hit .400 in the majors, and he certainly has the statistics to be on the Hit List. I personally never saw Heilmann hit, but I talked to Joe Cronin and Eddie Collins, who had both seen Heilmann in action. They were both impressed with him. In fact, of all the old-timers I've talked to about Heilmann, every single one has sung his praises.

He was a contemporary of Tris Speaker and Al Simmons and on two different occasions went head to head with them for the batting title in the American League. Nevertheless Heilmann is one of the least known of the great hitters to grace our top-25 group. He started slowly, but with that help from Ty Cobb he finished with a bang.

His greatest years were in the middle '20s, after he had finally learned to be a great hitter. According to Cronin he was a great line drive type hitter — on the same order as Joe Torre, the guy who used to be with the St. Louis Cardinals.

There's no question that there was a period during the '20s and '30s that produced the most gaudy hitting statistics in baseball history. Team averages and league averages soared, and records set then have never been approached since: Cobb, Sisler (twice), and Terry all had .400 seasons, while Heilmann came within a heartbeat of hitting .400 four times.

You can be cynical and disregard these hitters because of the sheer number of players with high averages. What you can't deny is the evidence. There's also no question that this was the biggest hitting era of all, which makes me believe that, generally speaking, there were better hitters in those days. Sure the ball was lively, but I don't know that the ball was any more juiced up than it is today.

There is one thing that's never talked about, though. There used to be a single seam on the ball, but in 1937 or 1938 they put a double seam on it. Now since that time there have still been guys who have hit 61 home runs, and there have been several who have hit 50, so you have to wonder whether the ball was livelier or deader as a result of the extra seam. But it's undeniable that there weren't as many good breaking-ball pitchers back in Heilmann's time, simply because — I believe — they didn't have the bigger seam to help them throw really good breaking stuff. And I think you'd find that any of the old-timers would substantiate that. They threw breaking stuff all right, just not as effectively.

Heilmann was a great hitter, but he was not a hitter in the mold of Mantle or Mays. He drove in a hundred runs eight times, but he did not excel as a home run hitter — even after the start of the lively ball era. He was still an impressive hitter, though, and once hit safely in ten consecutive trips to the plate, from June 16 to June 19, 1922.

On two different occasions Harry Heilmann battled down to the wire before capturing the American League batting title. In 1925 he refused to sit out the second game of a doubleheader to preserve his lead over Tris Speaker, and proceeded to go three for three. In 1927 the race was with Al Simmons, and again Heilmann picked up three hits in the second half of a doubleheader to win handily.

Ballpark Figures: The right-handed Heilmann played most of his career at Navin Field, later to become Briggs Stadium and ultimately Tiger Stadium. Left field measured 345' in 1921 and 340.58' in 1926; centerfield was 467' in 1927; right field was 370' in 1921 and became 370.91' in 1926.

Lifetime Stats

Years Played: 17
Games: 2146
At-bats: 7787
Runs: 1291
Hits: 2660
Doubles: 542
Triples: 151
Home Runs: 183

Runs Batted In: 1538
Bases on Balls: 856
Strikeouts: 550
Batting Average: .342
On Base Percentage: .410
Slugging Percentage: .520
Production: .930

18

Frank Robinson

Career: 1956-1976

Bats: R   **Height: 6'1"**   **Weight: 194**

Robinson is a proud and prominent name in baseball history, but when the name is mentioned most people tend to think of Jackie, who courageously pioneered the entry of blacks into the major leagues, or Brooks, who was probably the best defensive third baseman in the game's history. There's a tendency to forget about Frank Robinson, one of the top offensive ballplayers of all time. He was definitely underrated, although it's hard to see how he could have been so unappreciated based on his statistics and his accomplishments. As a fellow hitter, I sure appreciated what he could do at the plate.

Frank Robinson ranks right up there in my book with Mays, Mantle, and DiMaggio. He was probably as tough a hitter in a jam as Mays or Mantle or Aaron, but they came through a few more times per time at bat. He did hit .294, though, so he's right up there with those guys. There isn't enough difference in there to make any real difference.

But Robinson didn't play in New York; he played in Cincinnati and Baltimore, for Pete's sake. It makes all the difference: it's easy for the big-city media to forget about players in the smaller centers.

Robinson was a great right-handed hitter who won MVPs in both the American and National leagues — and he won the Triple Crown. Who else has done all that? He was an intelligent hitter who could adapt at the plate and hit according to the situation. It's true that his ballpark in Cincinnati (Crosley Field) was a good hitter's park, but he continued to hit well after he was traded to Baltimore, where the ballpark had larger dimensions. The Reds traded him because they said he was "an old 30." They couldn't have been more wrong. He promptly won the Triple Crown, and in his six years with the Orioles he led them to four American League pennants and two world cham-

Frank Robinson: the only man to win MVP awards in both leagues.

NATIONAL BASEBALL LIBRARY & ARCHIVE, COOPERSTOWN, N.Y.

pionships. He once hit a ball clean out of Memorial Stadium — the only player to ever do it. He had 586 home runs, while hitting just under .300 and knocking out 2943 hits. How many of today's players can make that claim?

I watched Robinson for four or five years after he'd been traded from the National League to Baltimore, and I saw just enough of him to know that he was one of the most aggressive hitters of the modern era. He played with a ferocity and a will to win that any modern-day manager would die for. And he could hit in the American League and he could hit in the National League. In his first year (1956), the big right-hander tied the major league record for most homers by a rookie, with 38, and went on to win the Rookie-of-the-Year Award. When he captured the coveted Triple Crown in 1966, he hit 49 homers, drove in 122 runs, and batted .316. He led the NL in slugging percentage in '60, '61 and '62 and topped the AL in '66.

On June 26, 1970, he drove in a record eight runs in just two consecutive at-bats — and as far as I know there's only one way to accomplish that!

And what desire he had! Writers call that an "intangible," but try to convince a battle-scarred second baseman that his hell-bent-for-leather slides are intangible. He was from the old school: intimidating, calculating, always looking for an edge. Sort of like a black Ty Cobb with home run power. He crowded the plate and openly defied the pitcher to throw inside. It's no accident that he tied the World Series record for most times hit by pitches in a game.

Factor in the important detail that he was an exceptionally smart hitter, and you know Robinson was something special. He knew how to hit according to the situation. He played mind games with the pitchers and always had them at a disadvantage because he was thinking two moves ahead — like a chess player. It's a facet of baseball that doesn't get talked about much, especially in today's game, but he was a master at it. Baseballic intelligence — Robinson had it in spades.

Frank Robinson was a winner. Aside from his impressive individual records, he led the National League Reds to a World Series in 1961 and spearheaded four Oriole drives to the American League flag. He won two World Series with the Orioles, in 1966 and 1971.

Following the tradition of his namesake Jackie, he became the first black man to manage a major league team. That event didn't get nearly the same attention as Jackie's arrival in the majors, but it was a watershed event in the evolution of the game, and they couldn't have found a more deserving person to take on the challenge. He had always been a great team leader: as a player he used to have those kangaroo courts to keep the guys loose during a pennant race. And he was a damn good manager too. He's done a very credible job in the past as a skipper because he has a good baseball mind. His name looks right at home among the trio of distinguished Robinsons, and even more at home among the greatest hitters in the game.

On June 26, 1970, Baltimore's Frank Robinson, playing with a sprained back, single-handedly destroyed the Washington Senators. Robinson hit two grand slams in two successive innings, the only player to achieve such a feat. The Orioles won the game 12-2.

Ballpark Figures: Robinson, a right-handed hitter, played the bulk of his career in two ballparks, Cincinnati's Crosley Field (1956-1965) and Baltimore's Memorial Stadium (1966-1971). Crosley Field was 328' to the left-field fence, 380' to left center, 387' to centerfield, 383' to right center, and 342', expanding to 366' in '58, in right field. Symmetrical Memorial Stadium provided more challenging targets for the slugging Robinson. The power alleys were 370', expanded to 385' in 1970. The distance was 360' where the seven-foot fence met the 14-foot fence and 309' down the foul lines.

Lifetime Stats

Years Played: 21	**Runs Batted In:** 1812
Games: 2808	**Bases on Balls:** 1420
At-bats: 10,006	**Strikeouts:** 1532
Runs: 1829	**Batting Average:** .294
Hits: 2943	**On Base Percentage:** .392
Doubles: 528	**Slugging Percentage:** .537
Triples: 72	**Production:** .929
Home Runs: 586	

19

Mike Schmidt

Career: 1972-1989

Bats: R   **Height: 6'2"**   **Weight: 195**

There are those players who make it to the Hall of Fame with their glove, and there are those who make it with their bat. I guess Mike Schmidt decided not to take any chances; he excelled in all phases of the game. He was the dominant offensive player of the '70s and '80s and he won ten Gold Gloves for his play at third. He played 2212 games at third base, third behind only Brooks Robinson and Graig Nettles at that position. There may be some room to debate whether he was a better fielder than those guys, but there's no question he was the best-hitting third baseman in history.

As a hitter Mike Schmidt was the power and thrust of the whole National League for most of his career. Schmidt was a big, powerful guy and he dominated the league in home runs pretty much on the order of Ralph Kiner. He did it longer than Kiner did, even though in many ways he wasn't as good a hitter as Kiner was. Schmidt had the league right where he wanted it, and the pitchers didn't have a clue how to handle him. That's a great feeling.

Schmidt finished his career with 548 home runs, the seventh highest total in major league history, and 1595 RBIs. He led the National League in homers eight times, in RBIs four times, in on base percentage three times, in slugging five times, and in runs scored once. Nine times he drove in over a hundred runs. He bested the league in the important statistic of production (OBP + SLG.) five times in his 18-year career.

Schmidt hit a couple of different ways during his career, and he was successful both ways. He hit to right center for a while, and then he changed his style and had some more great years as a pull hitter. That shows how he could adapt and how he analyzed what he was doing at the plate. He was an

Mike Schmidt was the power and thrust of the National League.

BETTMANN ARCHIVE

intelligent hitter who tried to put himself in the pitcher's shoes and think like the pitcher. He led his league in bases on balls four times.

Schmidt was National League MVP three times, one of only three players to achieve that level of dominance. His home run percentage (6.56 per 100 at-bats) is the eighth highest of all time. In 1976, at Wrigley Field in Chicago, he hit four consecutive home runs against the Cubbies and rang up 17 total bases in that ten-inning game. For an encore he homered in each of his next two games.

His best single-season home run output came in 1980, when he powered 48 and led the Phillies' charge to the National League pennant. He continued his assault in the World Series, batting at a .381 clip and chipping in two more homers.

His batting average is low — at .267 one of the lowest on the Hit List. He also struck out a lot more than he probably should have; almost a quarter of his trips to the plate ended up that way. But you can't deny his other statistics.

I talked to Stan Musial about Schmidt, and he agreed that Schmidt was the dominant power in his league for a long time. That's good enough for me.

Like many sluggers, Mike Schmidt was susceptible to strikeouts. He whiffed approximately once every four times up and stands third on the all-time strikeout list behind Reggie Jackson and Willie Stargell. However, he also stands eighth in home run percentage (6.56) and seventh in career home runs. Schmidt powered the Philadelphia Phillies to their first World Series championship in 96 years in 1980.

Ballpark Figures: Veterans Stadium in Philadelphia was part of the regrettable trend toward symmetrical stadiums. Schmidt had to contend with 330' distance down the foul lines, 371' to the power alleys, and 408' to straightaway center.

Lifetime Stats

Years Played: 18

Games: 2404

At-bats: 8352

Runs: 1506

Hits: 2234

Doubles: 408

Triples: 59

Home Runs: 548

Runs Batted In: 1595

Bases on Balls: 1507

Strikeouts: 1883

Batting Average: .267

On Base Percentage: .384

Slugging Percentage: .527

Production: .911

20

Ralph Kiner

Career: 1946-1955

Bats: R   **Height: 6'2"**   **Weight: 195**

For ten spectacular seasons Ralph Kiner was a home run hitting machine. And even though he didn't hit 500 home runs, he did hit 369 in a hurry in that abbreviated major league stretch. He hit them like he had a bus to catch.

After impressing the Pirates brass with 14 spring training homers, he broke onto the major league scene in 1946 with a league-leading 23 homers in his rookie year, and led or tied for the National League lead in homers in each of his first seven seasons. Only once, in his final campaign, did he dip below the 20-homer mark, finishing with 18 when a bad back forced him permanently to the sidelines. His 14.10 at-bats per home run ratio is second only to Babe Ruth's 11.76. That works out to 7.09 round-trippers in every one hundred at-bats, an amazing clip.

Kiner worked hard to become a better, more consistent hitter. Despite his home run crown, he had struck out over a hundred times in his rookie year and had a batting average of only .247. He wasn't content with those numbers. He studied pitchers and their deliveries much the same as I did. He even kept charts on each pitcher, and in that regard I guess he was ahead of his time. I kept my pitching charts in my head. Kiner also practiced with teammates for hours to improve his hitting skills. He was successful in cutting way down on his strikeouts, and he raised his batting average to a respectable level in the process. He made himself a better hitter through hard work and an intelligent approach to his craft. I respect that in a ballplayer.

A lot of people don't think he belongs in the Hall of Fame, but I sure do because he absolutely eclipsed the other power hitters in the league for a long time. In fact he devastated his entire league. He made a lot of noise over there,

Ralph Kiner was born to drive Cadillacs.

hitting 23, 51, 40, 54, and so on . . . and he did it for seven years in a row. His 54 homers in 1949 is the second highest total in National League history.

So you're damn right I believe Kiner belongs in the Hall of Fame. His domination as the biggest slugger in the National League for seven years cannot be denied.

It's too bad he wasn't on a better ball club than the Pittsburgh Pirates, who were pretty weak at the time. He didn't get much support. They pitched around him a lot and he drew a large number of walks, over a hundred per season on six occasions.

Even with the garden that they called Kiner's Korner in left field, it was still an authentic poke for a homer, and no one could ever say the park helped him that much, because he hit 159 of his 369 homers on the road.

Kiner hit over .300 on three separate occasions but couldn't maintain that level. He averaged over a hundred RBIs per season and led the league in that department once. He actually inspired the sentiment that home run hitters drive Cadillacs while singles hitters have to settle for Fords. It was his power that made him the highest-paid player in the National League. He drew the fans to the ballpark and they all left after his last at-bat.

Kiner was a disciple of the great Hank Greenberg, who had come over to the Pirates from Detroit in 1947 in the twilight of his career. Greenberg honed Kiner's natural ability and helped him to become a consistent power threat. He was obviously an eager student. You'd have to be crazy not to take advantage of a great resource like Greenberg. Kiner's best year came in 1949, when he powered 54 home runs and rang up 127 RBIs, both league highs. He hit 25 of those homers on the road that year, a National League record. That shows that he could hit anywhere.

When you start adding up all his statistics, Kiner was so devastating in the run production and power categories that nobody comes ahead of him, despite the fact that he has the third lowest average on my list. If his career had been a bit longer, who knows where he'd have ended up. With all due respect to the Ford Motor Company, Ralph was born to drive Cadillacs.

After Ralph Kiner had just deposited his best curve ball in the left-field bleachers, Chicago Cubs pitcher Bob Muncrief received some unsolicited advice from manager Frankie Frisch. "Never give Kiner a curve," admonished Frisch. "Throw him nothing but fastballs."

On Kiner's next plate appearance, Muncrief took the advice to heart, only to watch his first fastball land in an even more remote corner of the bleachers. When Frisch made his inevitable trip to the mound, a philosophical Muncrief indicated a somewhat tarnished silver lining. "Well, Frank, he hit yours a lot farther than he hit mine."

Ballpark Figures: Kiner, a right-handed power hitter, called Pittsburgh's Forbes Field his home for most of his career Left field was 335' away in 1947 and left center was 355'. Centerfield was 435', right center was 408', and right field was 300'. Kiner's Korner, also known as Greenburg Garden, was an area in left field placed there to enhance the home run totals of both hitters.

Lifetime Stats

Years Played: 10

Games: 1472

At-bats: 5205

Runs: 971

Hits: 1451

Doubles: 216

Triples: 39

Home Runs: 369

Runs Batted In: 1015

Bases on Balls: 1011

Strikeouts: 749

Batting Average: .279

On Base Percentage: .398

Slugging Percentage: .548

Production: .946

21

Duke Snider

Career: 1947-1964

Bats: L   **Height: 6'0"**   **Weight: 179**

In the 1950s, New York was blessed with a trinity of great center fielders. The Giants had the incomparable Willie; the Yankees boasted the mighty Mick; and the Dodgers featured the Duke of Flatbush, Duke Snider. All three were fine fielders and all three were the offensive kingpins of their respective teams.

Cozy little Ebbets Field was tailor-made for Snider, the only left-handed hitter in the Dodger lineup for most his time in Brooklyn. For five straight years, from 1953-57, Snider hit 40 or more home runs, a record he still shares with Ralph Kiner. For 10 out of eleven years, he hit 20 or more out of National League ballparks. In '53, he batted .336 and followed that up with .341 in 1954. In all, he batted over .300 seven times. He also led the league in runs scored three times (one tie) and in RBIs once. Twice he had the best slugging percentage in the NL and once he finished with the best on base percentage. He topped the league in homers in 1956 with 43. He sometimes struggled against southpaw pitching and he struck out more than he should have, but when he connected it was gone.

Like Mantle and Mays, Snider excelled in the Fall Classic, establishing new National League records with 11 homers and 26 RBIs in World Series play. In 1952 he hit four homers in a losing cause as the Dodgers lost in seven games to the cross-town Yankees. His best single season performance came in 1955 when his 42 homers, 136 RBIs and .309 average swept Brooklyn to yet another National League pennant and another post-season rematch with their AL nemesis. This time Duke was too much for even the powerful Yankees. He smashed four home runs to lead the Dodgers to their first World Championship.

Duke Snider: true hitting royalty.

NATIONAL BASEBALL LIBRARY & ARCHIVE, COOPERSTOWN, N.Y.

In 1958, Brooklyn's beloved Boys of Summer left the friendly confines of Ebbets Field for their new home in Los Angeles' cavernous Memorial Coliseum. In this converted football field, Snider's home run output immediately dropped from 40 to 15 overall and from 23 to 6 in his home ballpark. There is little doubt that if Snider had played out his career in Brooklyn, his home run totals would have been even more impressive.

Nevertheless, Snider finished his career with 407 homers, 1,333 RBIs, and a .295 batting average. His lifetime slugging average was .540 and his on base percentage stood at .381 for an overall production figure of .921.

With his rugged good looks, prematurely silver hair, and aristocratic bearing, the articulate Duke was true hitting royalty.

Duke Snider won the home run title with 43 dingers in 1956, the last Dodger to lead the league. The following year he had the doubious distinction of becoming the first player to power 40 homers while failing to drive in 100 runs on the season.

Ballpark Figures: Ebbets Field was the personal domain of the Duke of Flatbush throughout the heart of his career from 1947-59. During his time in Brooklyn, the left-hander saw the left field fence move from 357' -343'; left center was 351' from '48 onward; center field was 399' - 384'; right center was 352'. Right field was 297' from home plate.

Lifetime Stats

Years Played: 18	**Runs Batted In:** 1333
Games: 2143	**Bases on Balls:** 971
At-bats: 7161	**Strikeouts:** 1237
Runs: 1259	**Batting Average:** .295
Hits: 2116	**On Base Percentage:** .381
Doubles: 358	**Slugging Percentage:** .540
Triples: 85	**Production:** .921
Home Runs: 407	

Killebrew was a slugger, pure and simple. NATIONAL BASEBALL LIBRARY & ARCHIVE, COOPERSTOWN, N.Y.

22

Harmon Killebrew

Career: 1954-1975

Bats: R   **Height: 6'0"**   **Weight: 195**

Killebrew was a slugger, pure and simple. His career batting average was an anemic .256 and his single season high water mark was a modest .288 in 1961. He didn't have the speed necessary to beat out infield hits or turn singles into doubles. In fact, he stole only 19 bases in 22 big league seasons. He won no Golden Gloves for his play in the field. So much for what he couldn't do.

What Harmon Killebrew did as well as anyone who ever lived was hit home runs. He hit them high, he hit them long, and he hit them often — once every 14.2 times at bat to be exact. Killebrew hit 573 home runs in all, a staggering number for a big, right-handed hitter from Payette, Idaho — an area better known for garden variety taters than for the baseball kind. But Killebrew was no garden variety hitter.

They called him the Killer and it has to be one of the least accurate nicknames in baseball history. He was one of the nicest guys I've ever met in baseball and also one of the least colorful. A wonderful family man with a quiet, modest demeanor, the only thing he was capable of killing was the ball. He avoided controversy of any kind and, playing in Minnesota, his on-field feats didn't attract much attention from the national media either.

Killebrew debuted with a bang. In his first full season, 1959, the 23 year old hit 42 homers for the hapless Washington Senators. It was no fluke. He stroked 40 or more home runs eight times, six of those times he either won the home run derby outright (four) or tied for the honor (two). He won three consecutive home run crowns, 1962, 1963 and 1964. Nine times he batted in 100 or more runs.

When the Senators moved to Minnesota and became the Twins, Killebrew led them to their first pennant in 1965. He went on to bat .286 and contribute a homer in a losing cause against the L.A. Dodgers in the World Series. Perhaps his greatest single year came in 1969 when he led the Twins to the division title and captured the American League MVP award with 49 homers, 140 RBIs and an on base percentage of .430.

Killebrew was as strong as an ox. I remember they used to ask me who would turn out to be the better hitter, Killebrew or the other Twins outfielder, Bob Allison. I said, "Boy, I think Killebrew. I think he has a better swing," even though at the time Allison was probably considered a little better prospect, because he swung down on the ball and made better contact. But as far as I was concerned, not nearly as many good things happened as when Killebrew swung.

Despite his numerous strikeouts, Harmon's large number of walks enabled him to finish with a very respectable on base percentage of .379. He also drove in an impressive 1584 runs.

Believe it or not, Killebrew was discovered by a politician. Republican senator Herman Welder was a friend of Senators' owner Clark Griffith and convinced him to take a closer look at this native son of Idaho. When Killebrew retired in 1975 he had more home runs than any American Leaguer except Babe Ruth. It's too bad all politicians can't be as visionary.

The 1963 Minnesota Twins' outfield of Harmon Killebrew, Bob Allison and Jimmie Hall totaled 113 homers. Killebrew headed up the longball parade with a league-leading 45 four-baggers, Allison contributed 35, and rookie Hall added 33. In 1964, Killebrew again led the AL in homers with 49. Unbelievably, he had only 61 extra base hits all season long — a lone triple and only 11 doubles.

Ballpark Figures: Griffith Stadium in Washington was home to Harmon Killebrew during his first few years in the majors. The stadium measured 350' to left field, 372' to left center, and 421' to dead center field. Right center was 373' and right field 320'. Metropolitan Stadium in Minneapolis, where the right-handed Killer spent most of his career, was 329'-346' to left field during his years there; the deep left center fence fluctuated between 402'-435'; center field was 410'-430', and right field was 330'.

Lifetime Stats

Years Played: 22

Games: 2435

At-bats: 8147

Runs: 1283

Hits: 2086

Doubles: 290

Triples: 24

Home Runs: 573

Runs Batted In: 1584

Bases on Balls: 1559

Strikeouts: 1699

Batting Average: .256

On Base Percentage: .379

Slugging Percentage: .509

Production: .887

23

Willie McCovey

Career: 1959-1980

Bats: L   **Height: 6'4"**   **Weight: 198**

Willie McCovey was one of the most feared sluggers in National League history. It's difficult to believe that a 6'4" giant known as "Stretch" could play in anyone's shadow, but for most of his career that was the case with McCovey. For 14 seasons, he played alongside that other Willie, the legendary "Say Hey" Kid, Willie Mays. Comparisons were inevitable and the charismatic Mays usually got the bulk of media attention. That was OK with McCovey. He was content to do his job on the field and then retreat from public view. The fans in San Francisco loved him, though, because he was one of their own, whereas Mays had brought his show in from New York when the franchise was moved west.

Blessed with a smooth, fluid swing, McCovey led the National League in home runs three times: in 1963 with 44, in '68 with 36, and in '69 with 45. In 1969 he was a one-man wrecking crew, batting .320 and driving in a league-best 126 runs to capture the league MVP award and two-thirds of the Triple Crown. Seven times he had 30 or more home runs, finishing his career with 521, the same total as me. Eighteen of those homers were grand slams, a National League record.

Willie McCovey absolutely dominated his era. He broke in with a .354 average, capturing the 1959 Rookie of the Year Award. Pitchers must have been shaking in their cleats as they looked in at this glowering presence. In many ways he was a much more imposing figure than diminutive Mel Ott, who finished higher on our list and gets so much more attention.

Like many sluggers, McCovey didn't concede with two strikes and often went down swinging. He was seldom cheated though. Even when he missed, he put on a show for the fans with that 38 ounce bat of his. McCovey played

Willie McCovey, one of the most feared sluggers in National League History.

NATIONAL BASEBALL LIBRARY & ARCHIVE, COOPERSTOWN, N.Y.

for 22 years and did a lot of damage despite a relatively low .270 batting average.

I still remember that frozen rope he hit to Yankee shortstop Bobby Richardson to end the 1962 World Series. The Hall of Famer wasn't cheated on that one either, claiming it was the hardest ball he ever hit.

On the advice of Ted Williams, Willie McCovey eventually forsook his heavy 38 oz. bat for a whippier 34 oz. model.

Ballpark Figures: Left-hander Stretch McCovey's home for most of his career was San Francisco's Candlestick Park. Candlestick's left field fence was 330' feet away until '68 when it was extended to 335'; center field was 410' from 1961 onward; and right center was 375'. Right field was 330' until moved back to 335' in 1968.

Lifetime Stats

Years Played: 22
Games: 2588
At-bats: 8197
Runs: 1229
Hits: 2211
Doubles: 353
Triples: 46
Home Runs: 521

Runs Batted In: 1555
Bases on Balls: 1345
Strikeouts: 1550
Batting Average: .270
On Base Percentage: .377
Slugging Percentage: .515
Production: .892

24

Chuck Klein

Career: 1928-1944

Bats: L   **Height: 6'**   **Weight: 195**

Chuck Klein was a great hitter, but like Al Simmons he played in Philadelphia and was forgotten about. He was the Rodney Dangerfield of hitters but, even a quick glance at his record confirms that he deserves much more respect.

Chuck Klein was one of the premier hitters at the beginning of the lively ball era and, playing in the Baker Bowl, his home park for much of his career in Philly, he had a great advantage. It was a little bandbox of a ballpark and it probably helped him to hit 300 home runs, but it doesn't take away from his talent. You have to take advantage of every opportunity that presents itself, and Klein certainly did that.

Throughout my whole life as a hitter, I sought out the knowledgeable people in baseball and grilled them about hitting. I was always asking questions and I could be fairly persistent. Some might say relentless. In all that time I never heard one guy who didn't say that Chuck Klein belonged in the top echelon of hitters. Even though I didn't actually see him play, all of his fellow National Leaguers loved his hitting.

He really exploded onto the scene in 1929, his first full season. As the Stock Market crashed, Klein's stock rose to record heights. That year he hit .356 with 145 RBIs and a league-leading 43 home runs. He won the home run title four times and the batting title once, with .368 in 1933. In 1930 he joined the league-wide hitting orgy with 40 homers, a .386 batting average, and 170 RBIs. Significantly, he didn't lead the league in any of those categories in that notorious year — which should tell you something.

He won the MVP award in 1932 with 38 homers, 137 RBIs, and a .348 mark, and for an encore he won the Triple Crown in 1933 with 28 HRs,

Chuck Klein was one of the premiere hitters at the beginning of the lively ball era.

NATIONAL BASEBALL LIBRARY & ARCHIVE, COOPERSTOWN, N.Y.

120 RBIs, and a .368 average. Not surprisingly, those five years were the best he ever managed. If he could have sustained those numbers over his 17-year career, they'd have built an extra wing on the Hall of Fame to house his memorabilia.

My only reservation about Klein is that he didn't dominate the league for an extended period the way, for example, Mike Schmidt did during his career. Still, 300 home runs and a .320 average can't be denied.

When Chuck Klein was traded to Chicago for a brief two-year stint in the midst of his career, his offensive statistics fell dramatically. Some critics attribute the decline to his leaving the friendly confines of tiny Baker Bowl. Actually, his two years with the Cubs were plagued with injury, hampering his effectiveness at the plate.

Ballpark Figures: Left-handed Chuck Klein played most of his home games in Philadlphia's claustrophobic Baker Bowl. The left field fence was 340' from homeplate and, bordered by a 47' fence, center field was a 408' target falling away to 300' in right center field. Right field was a mere 280.5' away and featured a 60' fence.

Lifetime Stats

Years Played: 17	**Runs Batted In:** 1201
Games: 1753	**Bases on Balls:** 601
At-bats: 6486	**Strikeouts:** 521
Runs: 1168	**Batting Average:** .320
Hits: 2076	**On Base Percentage:** .379
Doubles: 398	**Slugging Percentage:** .543
Triples: 74	**Production:** .922
Home Runs: 300	

25

Josh Gibson

Career: 1930-1946

Bats: R **Height: 6'1"** **Weight: 215**

There have been many injustices in major league history, countless promising careers cut short by injury, scandal and war. Red Sox slugger Tony Conigliaro was a bright young star when he was struck in the eye by a Jack Hamilton fastball. Despite a valiant comeback effort, he was never the same aggressive hitter after the beaning. Shoeless Joe's career was shortened by the Black Sox scandal. He ended his life in disgrace despite strong evidence of his innocence.

As far as the war goes, I don't know a single player who has any regrets about fighting for his country instead of staying home to play baseball. Lots of Americans had their lives interrupted by the war. It may be an interesting and popular exercise to play the "what if" game but I certainly don't pine over the so-called "lost years" of my own career. And I know that Feller, DiMaggio and Greenberg felt the same way about their service in WW II.

The point is that at least we had a chance to play, and to test ourselves against the very best. Conigliaro at least had a chance to hear the roar of a Fenway Park crowd after poling one over the Green Monster. And while you can debate the fairness of Shoeless Joe's expulsion, the man still played long enough to leave an indelible mark on the game at the major league level. Certainly the war affected lifetime statistics for some of us, but the bottom line is that we still played major league ball.

Black players, up until Jackie Robinson broke the color barrier in 1947, were denied that chance. That, to my way of thinking, was the greatest injustice in baseball history.

There are countless black stars whose names should be household words across America. Stars like Cool Papa Bell, Oscar Charleston, Buck Leonard,

Josh Gibson's name belongs alongside Ruth, Gehrig, DiMaggio, Foxx and the other great hitters of the game. NATIONAL BASEBALL LIBRARY & ARCHIVE, COOPERSTOWN, N.Y.

and Josh Gibson. Instead, only baseball scholars and devoted fans know about these heroes of the Negro Leagues.

All my life I've been interested in hitters and all my life I've been hearing stories about the great Josh Gibson. Everyone who saw him said that he was the powerhouse of black baseball. I followed his career as best I could in those days and listened attentively when people brought up his name.

As far as hitters were concerned, Gibson stood head and shoulders above the rest. He was the "black Babe Ruth," according to those lucky enough to witness his feats. Just where he ranks on the list of baseball greats is much more difficult to say. The other players on my top 25 list are ranked according to a strict statistical system and can be directly compared with their fellow major leaguers. We have no such luxury with Gibson.

Because he never played a major league game, there is no statistical basis for comparison. In addition, the records kept in the Negro League are sketchy at best. We know that he played against many pitchers of major league caliber, but we don't know how many inferior pitchers he faced, how many games he played, and so on.

Much of the evidence to support Gibson's cause is therefore anecdotal. Coming from sources like Monte Irvin and Buck O'Neill, however, that's plenty good enough for me. Irvin and O'Neill, both exceptional players, are desperately interested in black baseball and are outstanding authorities on the subject.

This much we do know. In 15 games against barnstorming white major leaguers, Josh batted .426 with five home runs. We know that he had a power hitter's physique. At 6'1" and 215, with a massive chest and powerful forearms, he hit prodigious home runs. Walter Johnson once said that he "could hit the ball a mile." Some witnesses say he was also blessed with superior speed, others say he was only average. All agree that he had a boyish enthusiasm for the game and especially loved the challenge of stepping into the batter's box.

He and teammate Buck Leonard batted 3-4 in the Hampstead Grays lineup and were known as the Thunder Twins for their raw power at the plate. How much power? Leonard claimed that while playing a game in Monessen, Pa, Gibson once hit a ball 575 feet. Others talk of 600' drives. When his barnstorming, Mexican, and Caribbean games are factored in , some estimates of his home run totals approach the 950 range. He reportedly hit 75 in 1931 and 69 in 1934. Over a 17-year career with the Grays and Pittsburgh Crawfords, he maintained an average of over .350 and at least twice he batted

.400. His offensive barrage carried the Grays to nine consecutive Negro League pennants.

I didn't see Ruth play so I can't make that comparison, but maybe Gibson was a black Jimmie Foxx. I don't know how their hitting styles compare but both were right-handed hitters and both had powerful arms. Both hit for power and average. Also like Foxx, my former Red Sox teammate, Gibson was a big, likable, carefree guy who enjoyed life to the fullest.

After consulting with black stars from the Negro Leagues, I am convinced that Josh Gibson was one of the 25 greatest hitters of all-time. It was a terrible injustice that Gibson and other black stars were robbed of the chance to showcase their abilities in the major leagues. But baseball fans were cheated too. They were denied the opportunity of seeing some of the greatest hitters who ever lived.

As much as we would like to think that the game is pure, baseball history mirrors America's history. There are heroes and villains, times of greatness and times of shame. You can't erase those past injustices but you can speak out against them. That's why I am pleased to add my voice to those of O'Neil, Irvin and others and declare that Josh Gibson's name belongs alongside Ruth, Gehrig, DiMaggio, Foxx and the other great hitters of baseball.

Legendary Satchel Paige , one of the very few who pitched against them both, claimed that the two best hitters he ever saw were Josh Gibson and Ted Williams.

Ballpark Figures: Josh Gibson had more homes than a gypsy. The big right-hander spent considerable time playing at Pittsburgh's Forbes Field (1939-46) and Washington's Griffith Stadium (1937-46), both of which forced right-handed hitters to earn their home runs.

Honorable Mentions

Ten Who Came Close

The following ten hitters came closest to cracking the Hit List:

HITTER	AB	AVG.	SLG.	OBP	HR	RBI	PRO.
Honus Wagner	10430	.327	.466	.387	101	1732	.853
Bill Terry	6428	.341	.506	.393	154	1078	.899
Dick Allen	6332	.292	.534	.381	351	1119	.914
Earl Averill	6353	.318	.534	.395	238	1164	.928
Hack Wilson	4760	.307	.545	.395	244	1062	.940
Willie Stargell	7927	.282	.529	.363	475	1540	.892
Goose Goslin	8656	.316	.500	.387	248	1609	.887
Buck Leonard			—— no stats available ——				
Eddie Mathews	8537	.271	.509	.378	512	1453	.888
Eddie Murray	10603	.290	.482	.365	479	1820	.847

Some of those on my Honorable Mention list came very close to making the top 25, and I agonized over some of the choices right up to the last minute. In the end, however, it's important to differentiate between great hitters for average, great sluggers, and those select few who combined both facets of hitting. Some of those on the Honorable Mention list were great sluggers and some were great hitters for average, but few were both.

The slugger is a power hitter who sacrifices getting on base by striking out more in his pursuit of the long ball. As a result, some of these guys' low on base percentages play a major role in their not making our top 25. On the other hand, some great "average" hitters failed to make the Hit List because they did not hit for power like they should have. In Bill Terry you've got a .400 hitter, for Pete's sake, who is not in our top 25 because he failed to hit home runs during the lively ball era. A lot of his contemporaries hit marginally more homers than Terry did in the '20s and early '30s. In fact Terry's career roughly paralleled Babe Ruth's peak years, and yet Ruth hit 365 more homers than Terry during the same time span and under similar conditions. It's one thing for Honus Wagner to hit only 101 homers over a 21-year career in the dead ball era, but it's quite another to fail to hit the long ball in the lively ball era.

The greatest hitters are those who succeeded in combining slugging and hitting for average. It's not necessarily true that you have to sacrifice one for the other. Look at Hornsby, and Foxx and Gehrig. If you've got the ability to get the bat on the ball, then you can still take care of yourself pretty nicely after two strikes, so why not take advantage of what you've got on a given day? There may be a pitcher on the mound who looks like he's throwing you beachballs. Why not take a little liberty and go for the downs against that guy? Boggs and Brett are both good examples. They both could hit with two strikes. Sometimes you've got to concede with two strikes, but hell, Boggs concedes all the time.

With some pitchers I faced, I'd say to myself, "I don't care if he has two strikes on me," I was still looking to hit the long ball. I might have to hit a tougher pitch but I wasn't worried about that against certain guys. (Of course, against some pitchers I didn't want any strikes against me.) A great hitter should be able to assess the situation and hit accordingly. The 25 hitters on my Hit List, to a greater degree, did it all!

Following are thumbnail sketches of the ten who came close to cracking the list.

Honus Wagner

Career: 1897-1917

Bats: R　　　　　**Height: 5'11"**　　　　　**Weight: 200**

First came Ty Cobb, Honus Wagner was second, and then came the Babe. That's the order in which these three players were voted into the Hall of Fame in Cooperstown when it first opened its doors in 1936. If it's true that a man is known by the company he keeps, that should be all you need to know about Wagner, the man they called the Flying Dutchman.

In 1912, no less an authority than the legendary John McGraw said that Wagner possessed "the quickest baseball brain I have ever observed" and picked him over Cobb and Lojoie as the greatest player ever.

His name is synonymous with old time baseball and his baseball card is the most valuable piece of cardboard on earth. As I've said elsewhere in this book it is very difficult to compare players across eras but Honus Wagner towered over most players of his or any other time.

By today's standards he wasn't built like a shortstop. Awkward in appearance, the 5'11", 200 pounder would never be mistaken for Ozzie Smith. He is said to have had hands so large that they almost made a glove redundant. At the plate his power came from his massive shoulders and superior upper body strength. Perhaps his most distinguishing characteristics were his bowlegs and long arms. As the story goes, he was able to tie his shoes without bending over.

Was he the best player of all time as some claim? Certainly his name is the only one mentioned in the same breath with Ruth and Cobb. He was the best hitting shortstop of them all. You can pencil him into that all-time lineup without too much thought. I do know that he was not a Ted Williams-style hitter! At the plate he used an extremely exaggerated crouch, almost as if he were sitting in an easy chair. From all reports he wasn't too choosy at the plate either. Like Cobb, he gripped the bat with his hands apart and I'll be damned if I know how anyone could hit like that. In fairness, Cobb and Wagner bear about as much resemblance to modern day hitters as the Model T does to a Thunderbird. Both are classics of their day however. He was a line drive hitter with pretty good pop in his bat and could spray the ball to all fields.

Based solely on stats and comparisons with is contemporaries, it is impossible to keep Honus Wagner out of this book. Hell, his resume sounds like it was written in Hollywood. He played 100 or more games for 17 consecutive years. He captured 8 batting titles in a 12 year span and led the NL in stolen bases five times.

Wagner's career average was not in the same bracket as contemporaries like Shoeless Joe or Cobb, but .327 ain't bad. His highest individual marks were .381 in 1900 and .363 in 1905. He led the NL in doubles seven times and some would argue that this was the most important offensive stat of the period. He used his slashing speed to rack up 252 triples and led the league three times in three-baggers. His overall production numbers were dragged down at the end of his career, but he led the league in slugging six times, OBP four times and overall production seven times.

In his only face to face meeting with Cobb, Wagner came out on top, batting .333 to Cobb's .231 in the 1909 World Series won by the Pirates. Legend has it that he also gave Cobb a vigorous face massage with his glove when Tyrus slid into second base after taunting Wagner from first.

Wagner was a shy, gentle soul who was quite content with his $10,000 salary and never requested a raise. He played his entire major league career in Pittsburgh, just a stone's throw from his birthplace of Carnegie, Pennsylvania. He ended his career with 3,415 hits, 252 triples (a NL record), and 640 doubles.

Bill Terry

Career: 1923-1936

Bats: L   **Height: 6'1½"**   **Weight: 200**

Bill Terry was the last National Leaguer to hit .400. He batted .401 in that great hitters' year, 1930, equaling Lefty O'Doul's 254-hit record in the process. Despite his slugger's proportions Terry was a classic line-drive hitter. His .341 lifetime average is second only to Rogers Hornsby among National League hitters. Starting in 1927 the big left-hander put together a string of ten consecutive .300 seasons. He accumulated six 200-hit seasons and six consecutive 100-RBI campaigns.

They used to write that Babe Ruth was my boyhood idol. That's not true. As a kid I never really idolized anyone, but the closest thing to an idol that I had was Bill Terry. Now why was that? I was born in 1918, and in 1930 Terry hit .400, when I was 12 years old — and you know that's an impressionable age. That's the only reason I can think of for it. I look back now and I think, that son of a gun hit .400, and I did it too. It's almost eerie. I told Bill Terry about that one time during one of our bull sessions on hitting. He seemed pleased to hear it. I used to enjoy those talks because Terry was interested in the history of the game. We had a lot commiserate about too because even though he was well-liked by his teammates and fellow players, he was no darling of the press. Sound familiar?

Terry was a rough old fellow too. He was brutally frank — some would say arrogant. He certainly had a competitive drive. In 1934 he fanned the flames of an already bitter rivalry between his Giants and the crosstown Dodgers. Apparently he was asked about the pennant chances of the Dodgers and responded by asking, "Are they still in the league?"

Terry was smart, an intelligent hitter. But he was also a dedicated student of the game and a born leader, as his later managerial career suggests. "Memphis Bill," as they called him, led the Giants to three National League pennants during his years at the helm, winning the World Series in 1933. After his retirement those baseball smarts translated into financial smarts, as Terry parlayed his bravado into big money in the oil business.

He used to chew me out because I wouldn't go to the Hall of Fame induction ceremonies every year. I never used to go to Hall of Fame functions. I was inducted and then I moved right out of town. I should have stayed there and enjoyed myself and had a hell of a time; but I didn't. Bill Terry convinced me that I was missing out on a lot.

I still haven't changed that much in that regard, despite what everyone might think, but I do appreciate things a little bit more now. I appreciate being with those old guys — great, great players. And they treat you like royalty. Hell, they treat you so well that you even think you *ssfs* pretty good when you get out of there.

When Terry hit .400 in 1930 it was the lively ball era, and Babe Ruth had hit 60 home runs just three years earlier. And yet, Terry was never a power threat, managing a meager 154 homers throughout his 14-year career. And he only had 1078 RBIs. That's why there was some wavering on his selection to the top 25, and why he was ultimately left off.

I never saw him play, but Cronin said that he was a great hitter and his record certainly indicates it, although his limited number of at-bats might be another negative factor.

His .341 average puts him in the top echelon, and a .400 season puts him in a hell of a bracket! You can't dispute the fact that there are very few hitters who have the statistics of Terry. In some ways his career parallels Heilmann's, even though Heilmann had superior production numbers .

Despite the fact that he had his greatest years when baseball averages and baseball production were the highest in the history of the game, Bill Terry was certainly one of the greatest hitters. Not in my top 25, though; let's say the top 30.

Dizzy Dean was an overpowering pitcher and completely fearless on the mound. The Hall of Famer had an Achilles' heel, however, when it came to Bill Terry. One afternoon, after Terry had sent three batted bullets past Dean's head, Pepper Martin decided it was time to offer his teammate some advice. "Diz," he remarked, "I don't think you're playing Terry deep enough."

Dick Allen

Career: 1963-1977

Bats: R **Height: 5'11"** **Weight: 187**

Dick Allen was like a light bulb that burns out under its own intensity. From the time he broke in with the Rookie of the Year award in 1964, he generated excitement wherever he played. Brother, did this man have some talent! When he was at the plate, he positively bristled with power and energy. He had a lively bat and when he swung that monster, he was capable of great things. I loved to watch him hit.

He marched to his own drummer and had his own personal demons but there aren't too many players I can remember who had more raw talent. Allen batted over .300 seven times, hit over 20 homers 10 times and over 30 six times. He won two home run titles, led the league in OBP twice and in slugging three times. In 1966 he hit 40 homers. He was selected to play in six All-Star games during his much-travelled career in Philadelphia, St. Louis, LA, Chicago (AL), Philadelphia (again) and Oakland.

Allen had a love of horse racing and a disdain for authority. He was a sensitive man who was stung by real and imagined slights, racial and other-wise. He felt that there was different standard for blacks and whites and he wasn't going to suffer in silence. He could be a thoughtful student of the game one night and fail to appear the next afternoon. You never knew which Dick Allen was going to show up -- or not show up.

When the LA Dodgers gave up on him after a one-year stint, Allen moved his act to the Windy City in 1972 to play for the White Sox. Playing under the easygoing Chuck Tanner, he finally put it all together, capturing the MVP award on the strength of a .308 average and a league-leading 37 homers and 113 RBIs. It was the kind of performance that he was capable of every year. He finished his career with 351 homers and a .292 average and the mind boggles at what this man could have accomplished if he'd been more serious about the game.

Earl Averill

Career: 1929-1941

Bats: L   **Height: 5'9"**   **Weight: 172**

Averill will seem to some to be a strange choice for inclusion in this book. In his entire career he led the American League in only two offensive categories: in hits in 1936 with 232 and in triples with 15 that same year. Nevertheless, from the time the all-star game was first instituted, he was named to the squad six consecutive times. He batted .318 lifetime, hit 238 homers, drove in 1,164 runs and scored 1224 runs in only 6353 at-bats.

I like Averill because he supports my contention that you don't have to be a muscle-bound giant to be a great major league hitter. At 5'9" and 172 pounds, Averill was a legitimate power hitter. He used his intelligence and timing to overcome his lack of size. He hit over thirty homers on three occasions, and twenty or better five times. When he went to the plate in the 1930s he was treated with the kind of respect usually reserved for more imposing physical specimens like Foxx and Gehrig. The Red Sox certainly respected him. In a 1931 contest, Boston hurlers walked him five times in five trips to the plate.

Averill holds the distinction of homering in his very first major league at-bat in 1929, the only Hall of Famer to do so. What do you do for an encore after that kind of debut? Well, in a 1930 doubleheader against Washington, he hit four home runs, driving in 11 runs on the day. Three of the homers were in successive trips to the plate and he just missed a fourth when a long drive went foul by inches. The following year he drove in seven runs in a single game and in 1933 he hit for the cycle.

Averill's career was cut short by a back injury related to a congenital defect in his spine but not before he had made his mark in Cleveland. When the Indians franchise named its all-time team as part of the 1969 celebrations of baseball's centennial, little Earl Averill was placed in the outfield alongside hitting giants Tris Speaker and Shoeless Joe Jackson. He does not look out of place in such lofty company.

Hack Wilson

Career: 1923-1934

Bats: R　　　　　**Height: 5'6"**　　　　　**Weight: 210**

Hack Wilson did some things on the diamond that no man will ever do again. He brief courtship with greatness began in 1926 when he batted .321 with 109 RBIs and a National League-leading 21 homers. It was the first of three straight home runs titles and four in five years. In 1927 he hit 30 into the seats, drove in 129 runs and batted .318 and followed that up with 31 homers and a .313 average the next year. In 1929 he batted .345 with 159 RBIs and 39 homers as the Cubs captured the National League pennant The stage was set for his epic year.

It was 1930, a notorious year for hitters (and pitchers), that marked the high point of his ascendancy and signalled his rapid descent into mediocrity. His record 190 RBIs in '30 stands with DiMaggio's 56-game hit streak and Maris' 61 home run season as marks that stand beyond the reach of mere mortals. In that same year, Wilson batted .356 and powered 56 home runs, a National League record. If he had been able to sustain, or even approach that pace for a few more years, he would have eclipsed Babe Ruth as the nation's #1 sporting icon. Unfortunately, after attaining this hitters' Everest, it was all downhill for Hack Wilson.

The very next year he managed only a meager 13 homers, 61 RBIs and mediocre .261 average. He rallied briefly in '32, stroking 23 homers, 123 RBIs and respectable .297 average but was out of baseball for good within two years.

At 5'6" and 210 pounds, Wilson must have been a strange sight at the plate, like a Munchkin with home run power. He wore size 6 shoes, had an

18" neck and boasted shoulders so broad that it looked like the coat hanger had accidentally been left in his uniform.

His downfall was alcohol, which he is said to have consumed in prodigious quantities. Some wags of his day say that he was a lowball hitter and a highball drinker. That is as good a summary of Hack Wilson's career as any I can offer. He came to the plate only 4760 times and hit 244 home runs while salvaging a .307 average. It would be easy to dismiss him as little more than a footnote to baseball history, but how can you deny 190 RBIs and 56 homers? He deserves honorable mention for that landmark achievement alone.

Willie Stargell

Career: 1962-1982

Bats: L   **Height: 6'3"**   **Weight: 220**

In many ways, Stargell's career is similar to Willie McCovey, who made the Hit List. They have identical production numbers but Stargell falls just short of the magic 500-homer club, finishing his career with 475.

Stargell won two home run titles, in 1971 with 48 and again in 1973 when his 44 homers and league-leading 119 RBIs gave him two legs of the Triple Crown. With a vicious swing, he could be fooled but he was seldom cheated at the plate. He was the author of countless tape-measure home runs, including two massive drives that exited Dodger Stadium. He reserved most of his most memorable homers for hometown audiences, however. He hit several over the old Forbes Field roof, and Pirate fans still talk abou the upper deck shots he hit at Three River Stadium.

Stargell was a born leader of men. Following Roberto Clemente's tragic death in a plane crash, he worked to reestablish the chemistry which is the marrow of any winning team. He was the elder statesman in the clubhouse, keeping a high strung young team loose and bringing them together as a cohesive unit and, more importantly, he was a leader by example on the field. In 1979, "Pops" Stargell led his Pirates "family" all the way to a World Series championship.

He earned the '79 MVP award for his 32 homers, 82 RBIs and .281 batting average. There were players with better stats that year but you can bet there was no better ball player. He continued to lead by example throughout the league playoff and the World Series, capturing two additional MVP honors in the post season. The last of his three World Series homers carried the Pirates to dramatic seventh game victory over the Baltimore Orioles.

Pitchers must have been shaking in their cleats as they stared in at this imposing figure twirling his large bat like a baton. He was a big swinger who struck out in record numbers but still managed a .282 batting average. His value to the team was beyond question.

Goose Goslin

Career: 1921-1938

Bats: L   **Height: 5'11½"**   **Weight: 185**

Success didn't follow Goose Goslin, he took it with him wherever he went. He won pennants with the Senators twice, suffered a severe arm injury, was subsequently traded to the St. Louis Browns, returned to Washington and won another pennant, was dealt to Detroit and captured two more pennants in 1934 and '35.

My old Red Sox teammate, manager and mentor Joe Cronin had played alongside him in Washington and he used to tell me glowing stories about Goslin. He claimed that in terms of sheer talent, he was in the same category as Lou Gehrig. As much as I respected Joe's opinion, I can't quite buy that claim. Certainly there is nothing in the records to bear it out. Goslin hit .316 lifetime with 248 homers and only led the league in hitting once, with .379 in 1928. He did drive in an incredible 1609 runs, and that's without a Yankees' supporting cast that included Babe Ruth, but it's still a far cry from the great Gehrig.

Goslin hit the major leagues like a typhoon, batting .300 or better his first seven full seasons with the Senators. He sparked Washington to their first pennant in 1924, driving in a league-best 129 runs while batting a solid .344. Goose and his teammates went on to capture the only World Series in Washington franchise history, defeating the New York Giants four games to three as Goslin contributed three homers. The following season saw the Senators back on top of the AL standings once again, thanks largely to Goslin's .334 average, 18 homers (a significant feat in massive Griffith Stadium), and 113 RBIs. In the '25 World Series against Pittsburgh, he added another three homers in a losing cause.

As the Senators fortunes began to dip, Goslin continued to assault AL pitchers. In 1926 he hit .354, followed that with .334 in '27 and then won an epic battle with Heinie Manush to capture the batting title by .001 in '28.

Goslin crowded the plate and was completely fearless. He swung from the heels and went for the fences. Cronin said that he was never satisfied with his homers, always claiming that he hadn't gotten all of it. That's a power hitter's mentality.

It was a man named Bill McGowen who encouraged a young Goose Goslin to pursue a major league career. Goslin later returned the favor by convincing the powers that be to make McGowen a major league umpire. Ironically, McGowan was the plate umpire on the last day of the 1941 season in Philadelphia when I was going for .400. I remember him fondly because as I stepped in for my first at-bat that day he called time, walked deliberately around the plate and started dusting it off. He didn't make eye contact with me but he said, "To hit .400 a batter has got to be loose." Maybe it helped. Certainly I couldn't have been much looser that day. Thanks Bill. Thanks Goose.

Buck Leonard

Career: 1934-1955

Bats: L   **Height: 5'10"**   **Weight: 185**

Buck Leonard was the other half of the famed Thunder Twins of the Negro Leagues. If Josh Gibson was the black Babe Ruth, Leonard was the ebony Lou Gehrig. He's the only other player ever mentioned in the same breath with Gibson. The only one in the same class. Like Gehrig, Buck was a powerful left-handed first baseman who was often overshadowed by his more famous teammates. Also like Gehrig, his name is synonymous with endurance and class.

At 5'10", 195 lbs, the rugged native of Rocky Mount, North Carolina had only average size, but he hit for both power and average throughout his career. He was the captain of the Homestead Grays, where he played for 17 seasons, and was one of the most popular players in the Negro Leagues. He and Gibson led the Grays to nine consecutive Negro National League championships from 1937-1945 and he was named to 12 all-star teams during his career (All-star games regularly drew 45,000 or more fans to Chicago's Comiskey Park). In 1952, he was voted to the Negro Leagues All-Time All-American Dream Team by a blue ribbon panel of baseball scholars.

Based on available data, Leonard is judged to be a .342 lifetime hitter. He hit 42 home runs in 1942 and led both divisions of the Negro National Leagues with a .391 average in 1948. Conservative estimates suggest that he and his teammates averaged 200 games per season, 80 of which were league contests. The rest were considered exhibitions and were played against a variety of opponents from Moose Jaw, Saskatchewan to Venezuela to the Dominican Republic. There was no off-season for Leonard. When the weather got too cold up north, he moved south and continued to play ball throughout the Caribbean. He did this for 12 straight years. Regardless of where he played, the traveling conditions were usually deplorable and the salaries ridiculously low.

Many of the Negro National League games were played in major league ballparks — while the more celebrated "big league" tennants were on the road. For a number of years, the Grays' own "home" games were split between Griffith Stadium in Washington and Forbes Field in Pittsburgh, necessitating even more travel. In the early forties Leonard and Josh Gibson were informally approached by representatives of the Senators and Pirates about playing in the majors. Leonard, somewhat past his peak years, declined the offer, not wishing to compromise the chances of younger black prospects.

Leonard finished his baseball career in Mexico in 1955. It is estimated that he played over 4,000 games in his 23 years of baseball. He was inducted into the Hall of Fame on August 7, 1972 and called it his biggest baseball thrill.

Like Gehrig, Leonard suffered from comparisons to his more famous teammate; however, being second-best to Babe Ruth or Josh Gibson ain't bad in any league.

Eddie Mathews

Career: 1952-1968

Bats: L   **Height: 6'1"**   **Weight 190**

Lou Gehrig's rising star could never outshine Babe Ruth's already established brilliance. Giant Willie McCovey's considerable talents were dwarfed by the charisma of veteran Willie Mays. Meanwhile, in the 12 full seasons that Eddie Mathews played alongside the most prolific home run hitter of them all, Hank Aaron, he had 421 homers to Aaron's 442, a difference of only 21.

Eventually, of course, Gehrig, McCovey, and Mathews were all outdistanced by their legendary teammates, the top three home run hitters of all time. It was Aaron not Mathews, however, who was the new kid on the baseball block in 1954, arriving in Milwaukee a full two seasons after Mathews had established himself as a bonifide star with the Braves. In fact it was Aaron who had to prove himself to the fans and media because Mathews already had 72 homers under his belt before Hammerin' Hank took his first major league swing. Mathews had arrived with a bang in 1952, hitting 25 home runs (a rookie record, since broken) and becoming the first rookie in National League history to hit three homers in a single game for the then Boston Braves.

Until Mike Schmidt came along, Eddie Mathews was the top power hitting third baseman in baseball history. For the first fourteen seasons of his career, he hit more than 20 homers a year. In ten of those seaons he topped the thirty homer mark, including nine in a row from 1953-1961, and four times he hit 40 or more. He led the National League in four-baggers twice, with 47 in 1953 and again in 1959 with 46. His final total of 512 earned him membership in one of baseball's most exclusive circles, the 500-Homer Club. His landmark 500th came off Hall of Fame fireballer Juan Marichal in 1967 when Mathews was with the Houston Astros.

The popular Mathews was a key member of the Milwaukee pennant winners of '57 and '58. He and Aaron combined for 76 homers during the '57 season (Mathews had 32 and Aaron 44) and 61 the following year (Mathews 31, Aaron 30). With a total of 863 round-trippers as teammates, the Aaron-Mathews combo was the most lethal in baseball history, surpassing even Ruth-Gehrig (772) and Mays-McCovey (800).

Mathews lifetime average was only .271 but he managed three .300 seasons and batted .290 or better five times. He drove in over 100 runs five times and 90 or more 10 times, finishing with a grand total of 1453 RBIs. His value to the Braves was enhanced by his ability to draw walks. Batting third in the lineup in front of Aaron, he led the National League in bases on balls four times and topped the 100 walk mark on five occasions. He led the league in OBP in 1963. With Aaron batting clean-up, little wonder he also scored 1509 runs in his career.

Mathews was renowned for his long-distance homers. His very first major league home run cleared the 50' right-field wall at Philadelphia's Shibe Park, almost 400' from home plate. At old Crosley Field in Cincinnati, he hit a rising line drive deep into the center field bleachers.

Lou Gehrig, Willie McCovey and Eddie Mathews: three of the greatest power hitters who ever lived. Despite their own Hall of Fame credentials, their names will forever be linked with baseball's immortal trio of home run kings. Fittingly, Mathews was manger of the Atlanta Braves in 1974 when Aaron made baseball history with his 715th home run.

Eddie Murray

Career: 1977-

Bats: L & R   **Height: 6'2"**   **Weight: 224**

Eddie Murray is one of the greatest switch hitters in baseball history. He's not quite in Mickey Mantle's class, but he's shown amazing consistency since he entered the majors in 1977. Although known primarily as a power hitter, he has actually achieved the .300 mark seven times in his career.

Murray has topped the 100-RBI mark six times and averaged over 100 for his first 11 seasons. He exceeded the 90-RBI mark 12 times and hasn't driven in less than 75 runs in his entire 19-year (and counting) career. In 15 of those 19 years, he's surpassed the 20-home run barrier and five times he's hit 30 four-baggers or more. He tied for the American League lead in RBIs in the strike-shortened 1981 campaign and won the home run derby that same year with 22.

Murray's best all-around hitting year came in 1990 in Los Angeles, a year after he had been dealt from Baltimore to the Dodgers. After struggling in his first season in the senior circuit, he bounced back with a .330 average, 26 homers and 95 RBIs against NL pitching.

He batted .323 for Cleveland in 1995 and slugged at a .516 pace. He also contributed 21 homers and 82 RBIs to the Indians pennant drive.

He lacks speed and his production numbers fall far short of others on the Honorable Mention list but his ability to hit from either side adds to his offensive value. He already has more than 3,000 hits and is rapidly closing in on 500 home runs, a double whammy which will put him in very select company indeed.

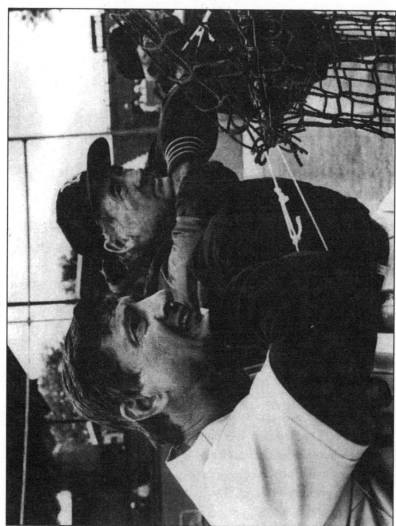

Yaz and Ted: together they stroked 1073 home runs for the Red Sox. AP/WIDE WORLD PHOTOS

At the advanced hitter's age of 40-plus, he's still having great years. He's a sure bet for the Hall of Fame.

Some Who Should Have Been Better

Some people will say that I'm too critical of hitters, and certainly it bothers me when a young player comes into the Majors loaded with natural talent and doesn't live up to his potential. Sometimes those guys turn out to be fine players, and some have even made it to the Hall of Fame, but to my mind they could have been even better.

Sometimes, of course, fate intervenes, and through no fault of his own, a player is robbed of the opportunity to show what he can do. Here are some notable hitters who fell just short of their potential for a variety of reasons:

- Carl Yastrzemski — Yastrzemski was a grinder, and I saw that when I first went to spring training with him. I said, "Boy, this guy is all coiled up. He's like a spring." And you can read where I said that if you want to look it up. I said that I liked his intensity. Yaz was an experimental guy with his style, with his bat. He could never convince himself what was good and when he was doing it right. And he couldn't convince himself when something was wrong. He changed a lot. Hell, at one point he had his hands way up in the goddamn air. How are you going to swing from there? I told him that as an opposing manager with Texas when he was in a bad slump. "First, get your hands down." And then finally, before he quit, I was up with the Red Sox, helping them with spring training, and he said to me, "Ted, I'm going to drop my hands," and I just said, "That's good."

  Yaz wasn't as smart as he should have been. Let me give you an example. The Red Sox were playing the Yankees in that 1978 playoff game where Bucky Dent hit the home run to win it for New York. The Yankees had Ron Guidry, the crafty little left-hander with the great fastball, pitching for them. Guidry had an outstanding year with a 25-3 record and a microscopic 1.74 ERA. He was a good little pitcher with a good hummin' little fastball, and he also threw a good slider.

  Before the game Yastrzemski came up to me and he said, "I'm going to look for this guy's slider today." "Bullshit," I said. "Look for the fastball. Hit the fastball."

First time up Carl got a home run on the fastball. Now you can talk to Yastrzemski and say that he's getting jammed and now he should look for the slider. Cripes, they've been throwing fastballs to him all day long, and sure Guidry might still come back with it, but he's almost guaranteed of a slider if Guidry's whistled a couple of fastballs by him. But he was still thinking fastball and he popped up to end the game. He didn't know how to make those adjustments during the game. That's just one concrete example of his baseballic thinking. It shows a tendency, a lack of proper thinking.

I never played with Yaz, but Bobby Doerr said he had the best single year Bobby ever saw, and Bobby played with me for ten years! In 1967 Yaz had a great year: he hit 44 home runs, 121 RBIs, and a .326 average to win the Triple Crown. That shows you the kind of talent he had and what he was capable of doing. He did everything for the Red Sox that year: if they needed a clutch hit or a stolen base, he got it; if the situation called for a ninth-inning home run, he hit it; if they needed a great game-saving catch, he made it. For that one year, he was Babe Ruth, Ty Cobb and Honus Wagner rolled into one. But one year doesn't do it. Yaz had desire and he had a great body and he had longevity. And I've told you what he was missing as a hitter. He wasn't as smart as he should have been, and he never knew when he was doing it right.

- Pete Reiser — You might not have heard quite so much about Stan Musial if Pete Reiser hadn't gotten hurt, because Reiser was a switch-hitter who could run like hell, hit .343 in his first full season in the big leagues, and was a super player. He might have given Musial a run for his money over in the National League. He just might have been a better player than Musial or Rose or anybody over there.

A lot of people who saw him in his first couple of years thought he was the best player in the league. Then fate intervened and he became a victim of his all-out style of play. He ran into the fence four or five times. He practically knocked his brains out once. Then he knocked them out again, and at the end he was getting almost punchy.

He hung on for ten seasons and finished with a .295 average, but he could have been a great one. He was a coach when I came to the big leagues, and by God, I had a lot of respect for him.

- Joe (Ducky) Medwick — Medwick was another guy who was a hell of a player and was destined for greatness. Then in 1941 he was beaned by Bob Bowman. The difference was that he put up some great numbers before he got hurt. His statistics indicate that he deserves some consideration for my Hit List, even though they were dragged down after the injury.

He won the Triple Crown and an MVP award in 1937 with 31 homers, 154 RBIs, and a .374 average. His slugging percentage that year was .641, so you've got to respect that guy. He finished his career with a .324 average, but he was never the same after the beaning.

- George Brett — Physically, Brett had all the tools to be a glorious hitter, but in his mental approach to the game he always lacked something for me. I certainly don't consider him an outstanding hitter. He's one of those guys who might not always have been as serious about the game as he could have been.

- Fred Lynn — Lynn had so much going for him when he came up to the Red Sox in 1975. I only wish something could have motivated him a little more — but he was a hard guy to motivate. Nothing stirred him up. He was content to have a pretty good year and go to the beach. He didn't have that little extra, despite his natural talent. He didn't have what Yastrzemski had: intensity.

  You hate to see young guys blowing the one chance they'll have. In 25 years they'll say, "Well, God, I wish I'd done just a little bit better." But that's life. I can look back on my own career and have regrets.

- Al Kaline — I used to talk a lot about hitting with Kaline when he came up. He had everything to be an outstanding player. He led the American League in hitting in his third year, 1955, with a .340 average, but he never led it again. Now something has got to be wrong there. Either he didn't catch up with the pitchers or the pitching finally caught up with him. That sure doesn't take away from his accomplishments, though. He was an all-round player who hit .297 lifetime with 399 home runs and was elected to the Hall of Fame. That ain't bad.

- Yogi Berra — Berra was a talented all-around player and one of the best-loved people in the game, but you can't put him on a list of the great hitters. His predecessor with the Yankees, Bill Dickey, was a better hitter than Berra, but Yogi was still a fine little hitter. He swung at some bad pitches, but not the bad low ones, only the bad high ones. And he was strong: he could get the ball in the air and really hurt you. It was hard to get the ball down to Berra. He never led the league in any major category but still hit 358 home runs and batted .285 lifetime.

- Charlie Gehringer — Gehringer was an early candidate for the list but he only hit 184 home runs. You've got to consider that: he's a .320 lifetime hitter but he didn't hit many home runs. A good hitter ought to hit a home run at least every 20—22 at-bats — somewhere between that and Ruth's once every 12 times up.

  So you look at Gehringer and he falls a little short in the real power department. He also played in a friendly ballpark; Navin Field in Detroit was a hell of a hitter's ballpark.

- Pete Rose — He was a bear-down son of a bitch and I'd want to have him on my team. He was a great all-around player, and you've got to give him high marks for his hustle and his attitude. But frankly, I didn't like his hitting at all. Rose had no power. You know what Mantle said about Rose? He said if he hit like that, he'd wear a skirt. Mantle was a rare bird who spoke his mind, and I agree with his analysis. There's no reason Rose couldn't have crashed a few more homers. When a guy gets the count in his favor, why not crank up and try to rip one? Rose seldom did. He was the first singles/doubles hitter to make the big bucks, and that was his trademark.

- Ernie Lombardi — Lombardi was a guy who could flat-out hit. He couldn't run a lick, and yet he still batted .306 lifetime and actually led the National League in hitting in 1938. Look his record up and I think you'll be impressed.

  There isn't anyone who saw Lombardi hit or who played with or against him who doesn't say, "He was as good a hitter as I ever saw." He finally got in the Hall of Fame, but it was a long time coming.

- Wade Boggs — Red Sox coach Ralph Houk asked me about Boggs in the spring of '82. I said, "He'll get the bat on the ball as well as anyone," and I was sure proven right there. I always thought that Boggs was capable of hitting 20 home runs a year, but except for 1987, when they livened up the ball and he hit 24, he's content with 10 or 12 per season. He has great bat control, but there's more to being a great hitter than that.

- Rod Carew — In 1977, when Carew looked like he was making a run at a .400 season, *Sports Illustrated* put the two of us on the cover. Carew didn't quite make it, finishing at .388, but he was a superb hitter for average throughout his career. Rod had a ton of ability but, as outstanding as he was, he could have been even better. He averaged less than five home runs a year and he was capable of many more than that. When I asked him about it he said, "That's the type of hitter I am." Well, he hit 14 twice. Why didn't he come back and do it again? He was good enough to do much better in the power department.

- Andre Dawson — Dawson was a terrific young hitter. Like Eddie Murray he was underrated as a hitter; both were outstanding. I liked Dawson's style. Unfortunately he has bad pins and it hampered a great career. There was a time when I'd have considered Dawson a franchise player.

- Reggie Jackson — What a hell of a guy to have in your lineup! He was a threat from the time the game started until the final out. He has to be considered one of the very best clutch hitters in the game's history. He's certainly been one of the great Fall players of all time; they didn't call him Mr. October for nothing. His World Series stats are incredible. He must like the cold weather because he's done some job in the Fall Classic. He struck out an awful lot, but when he connected he made things happen.

- Jim Rice — He hit as if he had two strikes on him all the time. He was as strong as a bull, but he was swinging when he left the bench. When you do that you hit the pitcher's pitch — and if you don't think the pitcher knows that, you're fooling yourself. He just says, "Hell, I'm not giving this guy anything to hit until I have to." The result is that you're hitting something tough all the time.

- Dave Winfield — He showed me that he was a fine player. At first I didn't think he could hit, but I was wrong, he could hit. He finally got his feet on the ground. I don't know how he straightened himself out, but he's a smart individual and I guess he figured it out. He realized how the pitchers were working him and he caught up with them. I respect a guy like that.

- Dave Parker — I was never impressed with him. A great big guy like that and he got more dinky little hits than anybody else I ever saw. How many home runs did he end up with? 328 in 18 seasons. He had a few fairly good years — but not good enough. I mean, the guy was 6'5", 230 lbs, ran well, and he had several sub-20-homer seasons. I wouldn't call that great.

- Roger Maris — He didn't have overwhelming career statistics but in 1961 he did something that has never been done by anyone else before or since: he got 61 homers in a single season. Somewhere along the line, they are going to have to recognize the fact that he hit those 61 home runs and that he did it while playing alongside one of the greatest players of all time — Mr. Mantle. I would be inclined to think that Maris deserves to be in the Hall of Fame.

Extra Innings

The Hitters: Left and Right, North and South, Tall and Small

For those who are interested in such things, 13 of my top 25 hitters were right-handers, 11 batted from the left side, and one, Mickey Mantle, was a switch-hitter. Twelve played primarily in the American League and twelve primarily in the National League. Because of the color barrier, Josh Gibson never played a game in the major leagues.

The location of the home states of the top 25 supports my belief that warm weather helps to cultivate hot hitters. Nine hail from northern states and 16 from the southern United States. Texas, Georgia, Alabama, and California lead the way with three selections each, while Maryland and New York each boast two. Other states represented are Pennsylvania, South Carolina, Oklahoma, Wisconsin, Louisiana, Ohio, New Mexico, Indiana and Minnesota.

The average height of our top 25 hitters is 6'1½" and the average playing weight is 196 pounds. Our tallest entry is Stretch McCovey at 6'4", our smallest is 5'9" Mel Ott. According to the official listing, Ott is also the lightest at 170 pounds while the heavyweights of the group are Ruth, Greenberg and Gibson who each tip the scale at 215. (Playing weight varies so greatly across a career that I suspect the Babe might actually be tops in this category too, however.)

Arguing Some Close Calls

Gehrig Versus Foxx

Gehrig versus Foxx is an awfully tough matchup. There are a lot of circumstances that go into a player's record. Look at Jack Dempsey in boxing: his critics say he never fought anyone — whereas there is certainly no doubt that Joe Louis took on all comers. The same applies in basketball. Despite Wilt Chamberlain's awesome statistics, critics say Bill Russell was a better player because his Celtics won more often. But there's no doubt in my mind that Chamberlain was the most dominant basketball player of his era. In the same way it's difficult to compare Gehrig, who was a left-handed hitter, and Foxx, who batted from the right side. It's always been tougher for a right-handed hitter. The ballparks favor left-handed hitters, and the fact that there are many more great right-handed pitchers also makes it tougher for righties.

Foxx was definitely the most productive right-handed hitter I ever saw; DiMaggio would be second in that department. Foxx hit 58 homers one year — and he didn't need short porches. He hit balls out of sight. I'd hate to say that anyone was better than Jimmie Foxx, but Gehrig's statistics suggest he was.

Hornsby Versus Cobb

Don't get me wrong, I'd love to have Cobb on my team. But in a comparison of these two great hitters, I'd have to pick Hornsby every time. He hit more home runs and he was right-handed, which, as I've said, is a disadvantage for a hitter. When it comes to a choice between power and average as criteria for a great hitter, I'll pick power every time. Throughout my career everybody told me that Rogers Hornsby was the greatest right-handed hitter of all time. He hit well in St. Louis, and then he was traded to the Giants and hit .361 there — even with the death valley that they had at the Polo Grounds.

But I'd never deny Cobb's place as the greatest competitor in baseball history. Cobb was a big guy for his time and he just terrorized the American League.

Gehrig has a slight edge over Foxx.

Hank Aaron: the Home Run King. LLOYD E. KLOS, ROCHESTER TIMES UNION

Aaron Versus Mays

Aaron was the better hitter, but overall Mays was equally dangerous. Mays was a great runner, with great speed; I wish I'd had his speed. And he was such an exciting competitor. For 15 years, all I heard about both Aaron and Mays from National League pitchers was "I don't know how to pitch to the son of a gun," and "What can we do to get this guy out?" Willie and Hank had the pitchers talking to themselves. It finally got to the point where Mays started swinging at bad balls, while Aaron was a little more controlled, but those two guys were in a league of their own. Their records say it all.

Ruth Versus Me

While comparisons with Babe Ruth are always flattering, there is certainly no doubt in my mind that Ruth was the ultimate player. He did more of everything, and you can't overstate what he meant for the game of baseball.

As far as hitting is concerned, he outslugged me .690 to .634, and while I had an edge in on base percentage, his overall production numbers are staggering, the highest ever. He also had the best home run frequency of all time. I'm quite satisfied to be considered in the same company as the Babe, DiMaggio, Gehrig, Foxx, and Musial. That's plenty good enough for me.

HITTING FACTS & FIGURES

by Jim Prime

Great Dates in Hit-story

- ◆ September 30, 1927: Babe Ruth hits record 60th homer
- ◆ May 25, 1935: Playing for the Boston Braves, Ruth hits his final three major league homers
- ◆ July 17, 1941: DiMaggio's 56-game hit streak ends
- ◆ April 15, 1947: Jackie Robinson breaks the color barrier, joining the Brooklyn Dodgers
- ◆ October 3, 1951: Bobby Thompson homers vs. Brooklyn to win pennant for the Giants
- ◆ October 1, 1961: Roger Maris hits home run #61 to break the Babe's record
- ◆ April 8, 1974: Hank Aaron hits 715th homer to pass the Babe on the all-time list
- ◆ September 11, 1985: Pete Rose strokes career hit #4192 to officially eclipse Cobb's long-standing record

The Exclusive, Elusive .400 Club

Alltime highest: Hugh Duffy, 1894 — .440*

Since 1901:

1. Nap Lajoie, 1901 — .426
2. Rogers Hornsby, 1924 — .424
3. George Sisler, 1922 — .420
4. Ty Cobb, 1911 — .420
5. Ty Cobb, 1912 — .410
6. Joe Jackson, 1911 — .408
7. George Sisler, 1920 —.407
8. Ted Williams, 1941 — .406
9. Rogers Hornsby, 1925 — .403
10. Harry Heilmann, 1923 — .403
11. Rogers Hornsby, 1922 — .401
12. Bill Terry, 1930 — .401
13. Ty Cobb, 1922 —.401

* A number of players prior to the turn of the century hit over .400. In recent times four players have come close to the coveted .400 mark. Ted Williams hit .388 in 1957, Rod Carew hit .388 in 1977, and George Brett reached .390 in 1980. Tony Gwynn was knocking on the door at .394 in '94 when the strike finished his challenge.

Hitless in Chicago

Righthanded Cub pitcher Bob Buhl went 0 for 70 at the plate in 1962, an unmatched record of batting futility.

The Top Five On Base Percentages (OBP)

1. Ted Williams, 1941 — .551
2. John McGraw, 1899 — .547
3. Babe Ruth, 1923 — .545
4. Babe Ruth, 1920 — .530
5. Ted Williams, 1957 — .528

The seat of power. COLLECTION OF BRIAN INTERLAND

Detroit Hit Men

Some people might find a certain irony in the fact that several of baseball's greatest "hit men" hail from Detroit, a city well-known for that particular profession. Hitters who spent all or a significant part of their career in a Tiger uniform include Ty Cobb, Hank Greenberg, Charlie Gehringer, Al Kaline, Rocky Colavito, Norm Cash, Cecil Fielder, Harry Heilmann, Kirk Gibson, Mickey Cochrane and Goose Goslin. And then there was Tommy (Hit Man) Hearns, a heavy hitter from another sport.

Two Great Years by Two Great-Hitting First Basemen

Lou Gehrig, 1931

46 home runs
184 RBIs
117 BB
.341 average
.446 OBP
.662 SLG.

Jimmie Foxx, 1932

58 home runs
169 RBIs
116 BB
.364 average
.469 OBP
.749 SLG.

The Best-Hitting Pitchers

The highest single season batting average in the American League by a pitcher was Walter Johnson's .440 for the Senators in 1925 (40 for 91). He was also two for six as a pinch hitter that year. Jack Bentley set the National League standard in 1923 with a .406 mark as a pitcher and went 10 for 20 as a pinch hitter.

Top Five Slugging Averages

1. Babe Ruth, 1920 — .847
2. Babe Ruth, 1921 — .846
3. Babe Ruth, 1927 — .772
4. Lou Gehrig, 1927 — .765
5. Babe Ruth, 1923 — .764

Making History the Hard Way

Jack Fisher gave up Ted Williams' dramatic home run in his last major league at-bat in 1960. As a follow-up, he also threw the ball that resulted in Roger Maris' 60th homer of 1961.

Rose vs. Cobb

	AB	R	H	HR	RBI	BB	AVG	OBP	SLG	PROD
Rose	14,053	2165	4256	160	1314	1566	.303	.377	.409	.786
Cobb	11,434	2245	4190	117	1937	1249	.366	.432	.512	.945

The Most Dramatic Home Runs

1. Bill Mazeroski, 1960 World Series

It was a situation made to order for heroics. The score was knotted 9-9 in the bottom of the ninth inning of the seventh game of one of the wildest World Series ever played. Bill Mazeroski, the brilliant fielding but light-hitting second baseman of the Pittsburgh Pirates, stepped to the plate and blasted a game-and Series-winning homer off pitcher Ralph Terry to defeat the heavily favored Yankees in the '60 Fall Classic.

2. Carlton Fisk, 1975 World Series

Catcher Carlton Fisk won the sixth game of the 1975 Fall Classic with a Hollywood style 10th inning blast "sometime after midnight." The image of Fisk dancing to first while willing the ball fair has became synonymous with the thrill of victory. Unfortunately, in game seven, the Red Sox became reacquainted with the agony of defeat at the hands of the world champion Cincinnati Reds.

3. Babe Ruth, 1932 World Series

For sheer drama, there is little to compare with Babe Ruth's "called shot" homer for the Yankees in Game Three of the '32 Series against the Chicago Cubs. There will always be great controversy about whether or not Ruth actually predicted his homer against the jeering Cubbies. But for those who knew Ruth — his hitting supremacy and his zest for life — it is perfectly in character. The three run shot was Ruth's second of the day and won the game for the Yanks. "I never had so much fun in my life," said Ruth.

At a fundraiser for the Jimmy Fund benefitting children's cancer research, renowned TV host Ed Sullivan, no stranger to introductions, introduces Ted to a necktie. Despite Mr. Sullivan's best efforts, it turns out to be the tie that binds.

COLLECTION OF BRIAN INTERLAND

4. Roger Maris*

Few hitters have challenged Babe Ruth in any offensive category, let alone homers. Roger Maris was one of the few. His record breaking 61st home run against Tracy Stallard of the Red Sox in 1961 came in the face of unbearable pressure from media and from fans who didn't want to see the revered Babe dethroned. They talked of putting asterisks beside his record because of the longer 162-game season (Ruth hit his 60 in a 154-game schedule). Maris may have lacked the charisma of a Ruth or Mantle, but he faced the pressures and he won. Asterisks be damned.

5. Ted Williams Bids Adieu

If drama demands heroes, villains and heroic deeds, then Ted Williams' homer in his last major league at-bat must be one of the most dramatic in major league history. Certainly it is the most theatrical exit ever performed on a baseball diamond. It came on a dreary September day in 1960 against Jack Fisher of the Baltimore Orioles. It came following a pre-game shot at the writers who were his perceived foes, and it came with no tipping of the hat to the fans. Williams' farewell shot was filled with irony and eloquence and heroics. Just like his baseball career.

6. Kirk Gibson, 1988 World Series

Drama often involves heroes overcoming adversity. When Kirk Gibson hobbled to the plate in the ninth inning of Game One of the 1988 World Series, he was the poster boy for adversity. With a strained hamstring and an injured right knee, he wasn't expected to see action at all in the Series. With two out and the Oakland A's leading 4-3, Gibson coaxed the count full and then flicked the next pitch into the right field bleachers. It was the inspirational shot the Dodgers needed, and although this was to be his first and last at-bat of the '88 Series, it helped win the World Championship for Los Angeles.

7. Hank Aaron Beats the Babe

Sometimes drama manifests itself in the achievement of a lifelong quest. For Hank Aaron this Holy Grail was Babe Ruth's seemingly unassailable 714 home runs. The quiet native of Alabama was the polar opposite of the charismatic Babe. For years he played in relative obscurity in Milwaukee and Atlanta while contemporaries like Mantle and Mays soaked up the media spotlight of the Big Apple. His 715th homer came amid racist taunts and intense — albeit belated — media pressures.

8. Bobby Thomson, 1951 National League Playoffs

Sports Illustrated has called it "the most memorable moment in baseball history." With the Brooklyn Dodgers holding a 4-2 lead over the cross-town New York Giants in the deciding game of the '51 National League playoff, Giant Bobby Thomson stroked a game-winning homer off reliever Ralph Branca. Even before he had crossed home plate, he passed into baseball immortality.

9. Reggie Jackson, 1977 World Series

1977 World Series. Yanks vs. Dodgers. Mr. October, Reggie Jackson, blasts three homers in three consecutive swings. This one's a package deal — you have to take all three. Love him or hate him, but give the man his due. Three pitches. Three pitchers: Burt Hooton, Elias Sosa and Charlie Hough. Three swings. Three dingers. World Series championship. Whew!

10. Ted Williams, 1946 All Star Game

Sometimes the times dictate the drama. This was hardly a nail-biter as the American League won 12-0; however, never was the world more in need of some non-military heroics than in 1946. The major leagues were just returning to their pre-World War II glory and the '46 All Star Game was the perfect rallying point — a microcosm of all the reunions that were taking place across America. Ted Williams, returning war hero and baseball legend, provided all the drama a war weary nation could hope for, including some comic relief. He walked in the first, homered and singled off Kirby Higbe, singled off Ewell Blackwell, and then hit one of the most unlikely home runs in history. Blackwell was famous for his blooper pitch that crossed the plate in a high arc. Most experts felt it could not be hit for a homer, but Blackwell playfully challenged Ted and the Boston slugger stepped toward the pitch and whacked it into the seats.

11. Joe Carter, 1993 World Series Winner

Carter became only the second man to win a World Series with a home run, giving the Blue Jays their second straight world championship. Carter's smash off Phillies' pitcher Mitch Williams set off wild celebrations across Canada.

The Rookie Ranks:

Highest batting average: .373, George Watkins (1930)

Most hits: 223, Lloyd Waner (1927)

Most RBIs: 145, Ted Williams (1939)

Most homers: 38 (tie), Wally Berger (1930) and Frank Robinson (1956)

Bases on balls: 107, Ted Williams (1939)

Slugging percentage: .621, George Watkins (1930)

The Best Composite Year in Baseball History

If you could put the greatest single-season performances together in one hitter, this would be his record.

61 Home Runs (Roger Maris, 1961)

190 RBIs (Hack Wilson, 1930)

170 BB (Babe Ruth, 1923)

.424 AVG. [post 1901] (Rogers Hornsby, 1924)

.551 OBP (Ted Williams, 1941)

.847 SLG. (Babe Ruth, 1920)

1.378 Production [OBP + SLG.] (Babe Ruth, 1920)

The Fortune 500 (Hitters with 500 homers)

Hank Aaron (755)

Babe Ruth (714)

Willie Mays (660)

Frank Robinson (586)

Harmon Killebrew (573)

Reggie Jackson (563)

Mike Schmidt (548)

Mickey Mantle (536)

Jimmie Foxx (534)

Ted Williams/Willie McCovey (521)

Ernie Banks/Eddie Matthews (512)

Mel Ott (511)

Aaron vs. Ruth

	AB	R	H	HR	RBI	BB	AVG	OBP	SLG.	PRO.
Aaron	12,364	2174	3771	755	2297	1402	.305	.377	.555	.932
Ruth	8399	2174	2873	714	2209	2056	.342	.474	.690	1.163

Never Too Young

Mel Ott was a mere lad of 20 when he blasted 42 home runs for the New York Giants. Lou Gehrig slugged 47 round-trippers as a 24-year-old first baseman for the 1927 Yankees.

Death by Baseball

The only batter to be killed by a pitch was Ray Chapman of the Cleveland Indians. He was beaned by the Yankee's Carl Mays in New York, August 26, 1920.

Out of Their League

How five great hitters did against the league average during their career:

	Personal Average	League Average	Differential
Ty Cobb	.366	.264	+.102
Joe Jackson	.356	.255	+.101
Ted Williams	.344	.260	+.084
Rogers Hornsby	.358	.276	+.082
Tris Speaker	.345	.266	+.079
Stan Musial	.331	.259	+.072

Did You Know?

♦ The 1961 New York Yankees trio of Maris (61), Mantle (54) and Bill Skowron (28) combined for 142 round-trippers.

♦ The Philadelphia Phillies' Del Unser once hit three consecutive pinch-hit homers (1979) - still a major league record.

♦ Wee Willie Keeler (1892-1910), who coined the phrase "Hit 'em where they ain't", practiced what he preached. The 5'4½", 140-lb. Hall of Famer once put together a 44 game hit streak and finished his career with a .341 lifetime average.

♦ Yankee Stadium, "The house that Ruth built," was appropriately christened with a Babe Ruth homer in 1923 in front of 62,000 fans.

- The first indoor ballpark, the Houston Astrodome, was christened by Mickey Mantle who stroked the first homer there in an exhibition contest in 1965.
- The '37 Detroit Tigers featured four 200-hit men. They were Hank Greenberg (200), Charlie Gehringer (209), Pete Fox (208) and Gee Walker (213).
- Incredibly, during Joe DiMaggio's 56-game hit streak, the Yankee Clipper didn't attempt a single bunt in 223 official at-bats. He batted at a .408 clip which included 16 doubles, 4 triples, and 15 homers.
- Sunny Jim Bottomley, who starred for the St. Louis Cardinals of the twenties, is the only man to face a lawsuit for hitting a home run. Apparently a fan was struck by a Bottomley blast and claimed with a straight face that the hitter swung "with the intention of creating a situation known as a homer." It's not known if the official charge was hit and run.
- When Roger Maris broke Babe Ruth's single season homer record with 61 in '61, he failed to receive even one intentional walk. Perhaps it had something to do with the fact that Mickey Mantle (who hit 54 that year) was waiting in the on deck circle.

The Longest Hitting Streaks

56 - Joe DiMaggio, 1941
44 - Willie Keeler, 1897
44 - Pete Rose, 1978
42 - Bill Dahlen, 1894
41 - George Sisler, 1922
40 - Ty Cobb, 1911

Hammerin' Hank

Hank Aaron hit 20 home runs in 20 consecutive seasons on his way to a record 755 homers in 23 big league campaigns.

Musial vs. Hornsby

	AB	R	H	HR	RBI	BB	AVG.	OBP	SLG.	PRO.
Musial	10,972	1949	3630	475	1951	1599	.331	.418	.559	.977
Hornsby	8173	1579	2930	301	1584	1038	.358	.434	.577	1.010

The Splinter and the Mick. COLLECTION OF BRIAN INTERLAND

Ruth: A One Man Team

In 1920, when Babe Ruth smashed 54 home runs, and again in 1927 when he stroked 60, he personally totaled more round trippers than any other *team* in baseball.

Great Single Years

Mickey Mantle, 1956

52 HR*
130 RBI*
112 BB
.353 AVG.*
.467 OBP*
.705 SLG.*

Ted Williams, 1941

37 HR*
120 RBI
145 BB*
.406 AVG.*
.551 OBP*
.735 SLG.*

Hack Wilson, 1930

56 HR*
190 RBI*
105 BB*
.356 AVG.
.454 OBP
.723 SLG.*

Carl Yastrzemski, 1967

44 HR*
121 RBI*
91 BB
.326 AVG.*
.421 OBP*
.622 SLG.*

*Indicates led league (Mantle's '56 season and Yaz's 1967 performance earned them baseball's Triple Crown)

Unlikely Hitting Heroes

While Hoyt Wilhelm was much better known for his pitching than his hitting, the knuckle ball ace hit a home run in his very first major league at-bat. It was the first and last round tripper of a 21-year career in which Wilhelm batted a meager .088.

Light-hitting Bert Campaneris raised the expectations of Oakland A's supporters when he homered on his first two at-bats in the major leagues. Bert will never be mistaken for Babe Ruth, however. The great field-no hit shortstop managed only 77 more dingers in his entire 19 year career.

Tools of the Trade

The Hitter's Hall of Fame at the Ted Williams Museum in Hernando, Florida displays game-used bats of each of the fourteen members of the exclusive 500-Homer Club. Also on display is a bat used by the most prolific home run hitter on the planet, Japan's Sadaharu Oh. The bats are on loan to the museum from collector Bill Nowlin. Following are the weight, length, and model numbers of those bats:

HankAaron	(755 HRs)	32.32 oz.	34⅝"	Louisville Slugger R43 unvarnished
Babe Ruth	(714 HRs)	43.20 oz.	35⅞"	Louisville Slugger
Willie Mays	(660 HRs)	34.88 oz.	35"	Adirondack Big Stick model M63
Frank Robinson	(586 HRs)	32 oz.	34⅞"	Louisville Slugger model R133
Harmon Killebrew	(573 HRs)	31.68 oz.	34⅞"	Louisville Slugger model S207
Reggie Jackson	(563 HRs)	32.64 oz.	35"	Adirondack 302 Big Stick model RJ288
Mike Schmidt	(548 HRs)	32.64 oz.	35"	Rawlings AD Pro Ring model MS20
Mickey Mantle	(536 HRs)	33.60 oz.	34¾"	Louisville Slugger model M110
Jimmie Foxx	(534 HRs)	32.96 oz.	35"	Louisville Slugger
Ted Williams	(521 HRs)	31.04 oz.	34⅞"	Louisville Slugger model W215
Willie McCovey	(521 HRs)	33.28 oz.	35⅞"	Louisville Slugger model K75
Eddie Mathews	(512 HRs)	31.04 oz.	33⅞"	Louisville Slugger model S2
Ernie Banks	(512 HRs)	33.92 oz.	36"	Louisville Slugger model S2
Mel Ott	(511 HRs)	32 oz.	33⅝"	Louisville Slugger Powerized
Sadaharu Oh	(868 HRs)	32.64 oz.	34¼"	General Sports Company, Japan Pro Number 5000 C-013 G2

(Note: Hitters often switched to lighter bats late in the season)

Babe Ruth's Record Year Versus Roger Maris' Record Year

Roger Maris, 1961

61 HR
142 RBI
94 BB
.269 AVG.
.376 OBP
.620 SLG.
.996 PRO.

Babe Ruth, 1927

60 HR
164 RBI
138 BB
.356 AVG.
.487 OBP
.772 SLG.
1.259 PRO.

Best Batting Averages by Position (Career)

First base: Dan Brouthers (.342)
Second base: Rogers Hornsby (.358)
Third base: Pie Traynor (.320)
Short stop: Honus Wagner (.327)
Catcher: Mickey Cochrane (.320)
Outfield: Ty Cobb (.366)

Most Runs in a Single Game

The Philadelphia Phillies and the Chicago Cubs combined for 49 runs as the Phillies squeaked past the Cubbies by a 26-23 margin in 1922.

Baylor Passes Pain Threshold

Don Baylor, current manager of the Colorado Rockies and formerly a DH-for-hire throughout the American League, passed previous top target Ron Hunt to stand alone atop one rather dubious hit list. Baylor helped turn Hit by Pitch into a legitimate offensive weapon, setting a major league record of 267 HBPs in 18 seasons. Ouch!

Whiffle Ball

Reggie Jackson struck out a record 2,597 times in his 20-year career.

"I am grateful and know how lucky I was to have been born an American and had a chance to play the game I loved, the greatest game." COLLECTION OF BRIAN INTERLAND

Hall of Fame Speech, Cooperstown, New York, July 1966

I guess every player thinks about going into the Hall of Fame. Now that the moment has come for me, I find it is difficult to say what is really in my heart. But I know it is the greatest thrill of my life. I received 280-odd votes from the writers. I know I didn't have 280-odd close friends among the writers. I know they voted for me because they felt it in their minds and some in their hearts that I rated it, and I want to say to them: Thank you from the bottom of my heart.

Today I am thinking about a lot of things. I am thinking of my playground director in San Diego, Rodney Luscomb, and my high school coach, Wos Caldwell, and my managers, who had such patience with me and helped me so much — fellows like Frank Shellenback, Donie Bush, Joe Cronin and Joe McCarthy. I am thinking of Eddie Collins, who had so much faith in me — and to be in the Hall of Fame with him particularly, as well as these other great players, is a great honor. I'm sorry Eddie isn't here today.

I'm thinking too of Tom Yawkey. I have always said it: Tom Yawkey is the greatest owner in baseball. I was lucky to have played on the club he owned and I'm grateful to him for being here today.

But I'd not be leveling if I left it at that. Ballplayers are not born great. They're not born great hitters or pitchers or managers, and luck isn't the big factor. No one has come up with a substitute for hard work. I've never met a great player who didn't have to work harder at learning to play ball than anything else he ever did. To me it was the greatest fun I had, which probably explains why today I feel both humility and pride, because God let me play the game and I learned to be good at it.

The other day Willie Mays hit his 522nd home run. He has gone past me, and he's pushing and I say to him, "Go get 'em Willie." Baseball gives every American boy a chance to excel. Not just to be as good as someone else, but to be better. This is the nature of man and the name of the game. I hope that some day Satchel Paige and Josh Gibson will be voted into the Hall of Fame as symbols of the great Negro Players who are not here only because they weren't given the chance. As time goes on I'll be thinking baseball, teaching baseball and arguing for baseball to keep it right on top of American sports, just as it is in Japan, Mexico, Venezuela and other Latin and South American countries. I know Casey Stengel feels the same way... I also know I'll lose a dear friend if I don't stop talking. I'm eating into his time, and that is unforgivable. So in closing, I'm grateful and know how lucky I was to have been born an American and had a chance to play the game I loved, the greatest game.

Two Views of Ted: From the Press Box and the Bleachers

Ted Williams feuded with both media and fans during his tumultuous years in Boston. Thirty-five years after his retirement from the game, here are some thoughts from representatives of both camps.

From the Press Box: A Defiant Tip of the Hat from a Latter Day Knight of the Keyboard

In my opinion, Ted Williams was the greatest hitter who ever lived. There, I've said it.

Ted's batting feats have become the yardstick by which all others must be measured. Any Red Sox fan worth a pinch of resin can recite the figures — 521 lifetime homers, .344 average, the last man in the history of major league baseball to hit .400. He also chalked up 1,798 runs, 1,839 RBIs and 2,019 walks in his war-shortened career while striking out only 709 times, an average of 37 per season. By way of comparison, Mo Vaughn whiffed 150 times in his 1995 American League MVP campaign.

Williams was American League batting champion six times, home run champ four times, RBI leader four times. He captured two Triple Crowns, a feat so rare that the last man to win one was Carl Yastrzemski in 1967. Ted was AL Most Valuable Player in 1946 and 1949 and could have legitimately laid claim to two additional MVP awards. In 1941 Ted hit .406 and still finished second in balloting to DiMaggio, who picked that season to put together his 56-game hit streak. In 1947 he batted a league-leading .343 and again lost out to the Yankee Clipper — this time by a single vote. It was later revealed that a Boston writer had left Williams off the ballot entirely. Even a tenth place vote would have made Ted AL MVP. Little wonder he had such warm feelings for the Boston press.

Ted led the league in runs scored six times. Four times he won the RBI crown; eight times he walked more than anyone else. Twice he led the junior circuit in doubles. He was chosen to the AL all-star squad 16 times. In 1960 *The Sporting News* named him player of the decade and in 1966 he was elected to the Hall of Fame. He lost five prime years to two wars and who can calculate what his career numbers would have been if that hadn't happened?

In the key statistical categories which Ted and I used to compile our list of great hitters, Ted Williams and Babe Ruth dominate. His .634 lifetime slugging average is second only to Ruth's and his career on base percentage of .483 is the highest of all time (Ruth is second with a .474 mark). His overall production mark of 1.116 falls just short of the Babe's 1.163.

Ted finished first in slugging nine times and had the best on base percentage 12 times in his 19 years in the majors. In 1941, the year he hit .406, Ted had an unbelievable .551 on base percentage. His top slugging mark was .731 in 1957 when he batted .388 and hit 38 home runs at the advanced (for a hitter) age of 39. If he'd had only average speed he would certainly have legged out enough infield hits to carry him to another .400 campaign and wouldn't *that* have been something?! In that same season he twice hit three homers in a single game, drew a record 33 intentional walks (that's what I call respecting your elders), reached base 16 straight times, and hit four consecutive home runs in four consecutive official at-bats. He won the batting title again the next season (.328) to help usher in his 40th year and bowed out with a .316 average in 1960 at the age of 42.

There are a million Ted Williams stories but here's one that shows what fellow hitters thought of "Terrible Ted". In 1946 Mickey Vernon, the fine hitter for the Washington Senators, was battling Ted for the AL batting title (which Vernon went on to win by a .353 to .342 margin). Instead of feeling elated by his accomplishment, Vernon was apologetic. "I stand by the batting cage just to watch Ted swing," he admitted. "It embarrasses me to think that I'm ahead of him. I'm not even in the same class with him." Such was the impact of Ted Williams.

Statistics aside, what really made Williams' hitting legend was his unmatched flair for drama. He had a repertoire of classic exits that would rival the most accomplished Shakespearean actors. At the outbreak of the Korean War he was recalled by the Marines where he would see active duty as a fighter pilot. He responded to the recall with a snarl and a game-winning homer in his last at-bat before a large and sentimental crowd at Boston's Fenway Park.

In 1941, Ted was batting .3995 going into the last day of the season — a double header with Connie Mack's Athletics in Philadelphia. Rounded off, this would have resulted in a .400 campaign. "Sit out the game," said coach Joe Cronin. "Save your .400 season."

"To hell with that," responded Ted. "I'll play." He played both ends of the doubleheader and ended up with a 6-8 day — and a .406 average, the last one over .400 on record. Just for fun he threw in a home run and a double off the loudspeaker in right field. (Decades later movie-goers saw the drama of that moment on the big screen when Roy Hobbs — Robert Redford — a left-handed hitter coincidentally wearing number 9, duplicated the feat in the film *The Natural.*)

For anyone foolhardy enough to still question his sense of theater, Ted Williams provided the ultimate performance on September 28, 1960 when he homered in his last at-bat. As thousands cheered, he refused to tip his hat to the Fenway Faithful. It was a final defiant, if misplaced, gesture to those he dubbed the "knights of the keyboard," the writers whom he felt had been so unfair, and in some cases downright vicious, throughout his career.

If this had been *Jim Prime's Hit List*, Ted Williams would have been acknowledged as the greatest hitter who ever lived. But Ted vehemently opposed any suggestion of ranking himself. For once he wanted the writer's luxury of relative anonymity and was content to let readers make such determinations. Well Ted, consider this Afterword to be the writer's revenge — a last defiant act by a scribe who happens to believe in his own heart and in his own mind that Ted Williams belongs at the top of any hit list. Ahead of DiMaggio. Ahead of the great Gehrig and the impeccable Hornsby. And yes, ahead of even the Babe.

A last defiant tip of the hat from an admiring Knight of the Keyboard: On Jim Prime's Hit List, you're number one. Take that, Ted Williams.

— *Jim Prime*

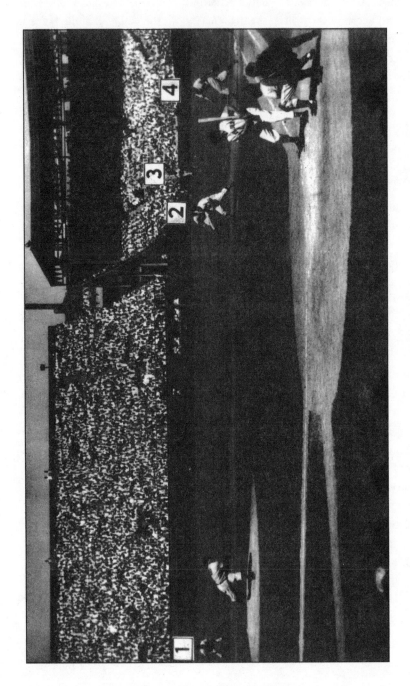

Ted battles the "Williams shift." There's only one infielder to the left of second base. BRIAN INTERLAND COLLECTION

From the Bleachers: A Fan's Perspective

Baseball fans employ statistics the way gladiators once used swords and shields. They can be brandished as offensive weapons to establish the superiority of a given hero, or as armor to deflect an unwarranted attack on your favorite player. Either way they are indispensable. RBIs, OBPs, BAs, HRs, SLG are all part of an arsenal that is polished, honed to incredible sharpness and kept carefully sheathed until the first challenge. You don't win many baseball arguments with sentiment or eloquence. That's why stats are the heavy artillery of baseball fandom.

In this battle of baseball stats, fans of Ted Williams and Babe Ruth are armed to the teeth. In the statistical category that Williams and Prime most rely on in this book, Production (combination of OBP and SLG.), Ruth finishes first with a 1.163 mark; Ted is second with 1.116. Ted holds the record as the all-time leader in OBP (.483 to Ruth's .474) but his .634 slugging percentage falls considerably shy of the Babe's unassailable .690. Ruth may have been helped substantially by batting ahead of the formidable Gehrig (#3 lifetime in Production) for half of Ruth's career.

There is certainly no doubt that slugging is important: producing runs is what wins ballgames and a double obviously better than a single in furthering that cause. From this fan's viewpoint, however, the primary task of the hitter is to get on base. Ted Williams always believed that a walk was as good as a hit and yet this key offensive category has been virtually ignored by baseball statisticians. A walk gets a runner on base, provides a scoring opportunity and often advances a first base runner to scoring position. Even an intentional walk — a tribute to both the hitter and the situation — can serve to rattle the pitcher and open the offensive floodgates.

To me, Ted's lifetime OBP is a very telling stat. He drew so many walks that when added to his lifetime .344 average, he reached base almost half the times he came to the plate. Even at the age of 40, Ted's OBP was an extraordinary .528, the fourth highest of any player in the modern era. In total, he led the American League in OBP 12 times.

Another key statistic which is sometimes ignored when discussing the great hitters is strikeouts. Strikeouts destroy scoring opportunities by ending an inning or removing the possibility of a sacrifice. If strikeouts were to be considered a negative stat and actually deducted from the overall offensive record of each hitter, the gap between Ruth and Williams would narrow considerably. Ted struck out only 709 times in 7706 at-bats, just over 9% of the times he came to the plate. Ruth struck out 1330 times in his 8399 at-bats, almost 16% of the time.

Sacrifice flies are not counted in today's game as an at-bat; therefore, a batter's average does not suffer if he contributes to the team effort with a sacrifice. Sacrifice flies were never counted against Ruth at any time during his career. On the other hand, in eight of Ted's 19 seasons, sacrifice flies were counted as an at-bat and an out, effectively penalizing the batter by depressing his batting average. Even in Ted's landmark year, he labored against this short-lived but unfair rule. If the six sacrifice flies he hit that year had not been counted, his average of 1941 would have been .412.

Ruth was truly a great all-around player. He was an astonishingly good pitcher and had he continued in that trade he would probably be in the Hall of Fame anyway. With 94 wins to just 46 losses, and a lifetime 2.28 ERA, he was already well on his way. On the other hand, Ted's one inning on the mound produced a 4.50 ERA and a curious footnote to baseball history.

For hitters however, there are four exclusive "clubs" to which one can aspire. The "500 Home Run Club" is perhaps the most obvious, but there is also the "3000 Hit Club," the "Triple Crown Club" and the ".400 Club." Ted is the only player in baseball history with membership in three of these fraternities. With his 521 home runs, two Triple Crowns, and a .406 average in 1941, he is a member in good standing. Ruth belongs only to the 500 Homer Club (and the 600 and 700 Homer Clubs too, for that matter).

Ted calls Babe Ruth the greatest hitter who ever lived and if Ted Williams says it I'll respect his opinion. But Ted sure as hell isn't far behind.

—Bill Nowlin, President and Founder of Rounder Records, is a
devoted baseball fan and a firm believer that Ted Williams
is the greatest hitter of all time.

ACKNOWLEDGMENTS

I wouldn't have gotten to first base on this project without help from a number of people. First among them was Louise Kaufman, who helped me get into the ballpark.

Thanks also to Linda Cann, Floyd Preston, John Henry Williams, Rich Eschen, Hank Aaron, Stan Musial, Pat Kelly (Hall of Fame Library), Bill Nowlin, Buzz Horan, Brian Interland, Frank Brothers, Glenna Prime, Bill and Karen Wilder, Don Bastian, Tom Bast, Holly Kondras, Kevin Linder, and Brian O'Donnell. And of course, Ted Williams, who, thank God, views persistence as a virtue.

— Jim Prime